LITERARY PUBLISHING IN AMERICA
1790-1850

PUBLICATIONS OF THE A. S. W. ROSENBACH
FELLOWSHIP IN BIBLIOGRAPHY

Proposals Relating to the Education of Youth in Pennsylvania
by Benjamin Franklin

Ex Libris Carissimis
by Christopher Morley

An American Bookshelf, 1755
by Lawrence C. Wroth

The Script of Jonathan Swift and Other Essays
by Shane Leslie

Bibliography and Pseudo-Bibliography
by A. Edward Newton

Three Americanists
by Randolph G. Adams

Printing in the Fifteenth Century
by George Parker Winship

The Cambridge Press
by George Parker Winship

Standards of Bibliographical Description
by Curt F. Buhler, James G. McManaway, and Lawrence C. Wroth

The Voice of the Old Frontier
by R. W. G. Vail

The Great Medical Bibliographers
by John F. Fulton

Bartolomé de Las Casas
by Lewis Hanke

Papermaking in Pioneer America
by Dard Hunter

The Appreciation of Ancient and Medieval Science During the Renaissance (1450-1600)
by George Sarton

The Books of a New Nation: United States Government Publications, 1774-1814
by J. H. Powell

Literary Publishing in America, 1790-1850
by William Charvat

Literary Publishing in America
1790-1850

by

William Charvat
A. S. W. Rosenbach Fellow
In Bibliography, 1957-58

PHILADELPHIA
UNIVERSITY OF PENNSYLVANIA PRESS

To
Arthur Hobson Quinn

PREFACE

These chapters are, in one sense, a skimming, in other ways, a condensation, of materials which I collected years ago toward a history of the economics of authorship in America. I had hoped to add a new dimension to literary history, but the dimension turned out to be too narrow. Literary history, no matter what the historian's approach, must be primarily concerned with literature. If the approach is wholly extrinsic, as mine was at the beginning, the product is likely to be sterile. Facts and figures about sales of books and incomes of authors are interesting—but not interesting enough, unless they specifically reveal something about the ways in which writers and their writings function in a culture. Similarly, the history of publishing, with which I became deeply involved, tended, like most specialties, to become an end in itself. Publishing is relevant to literary history only in so far as it can be shown to be, ultimately, a shaping influence on literature. I believe that it is and always has been precisely that, but literary historians have only superficially recognized the fact.

When these things became clear to me, I limited my study to those writers for whom both art and income were matters of concern, and whose work, accordingly, revealed the often conflicting pressures of the will to

7

create and the need to create for a buying public. This plan eliminated not only the private poets and the hack writers, but such authors as Thoreau and Whitman who, "public" though their purposes were, never succeeded in becoming professional on an economic plane. At the same time, in order to keep literature at the center of my investigations, I began working from the inside out—that is, from what the literary work itself could tell me about the writer's relation to society, out toward the reading public and the publishing economy which conditioned that relation.

In the forthcoming chapters, I have attempted to establish some of the background for such a view of literary history. The decades with which they are concerned, 1790 to 1850, form a coherent unit. The first date is that of our first national copyright law; the second is the year the railroads first crossed the Alleghenies. Without the first event there could be no literary profession; until the second, a truly national culture and literature was more of a promise than a fact.

Between the two dates, the literary profession was born, came to adolescence, survived a sickness which almost killed it, and reached maturity. Its adolescence was in the 1820's and 1830's, when the professional successes of Irving and Cooper, and of their pioneering publishers, Carey & Lea, were in sharp and illuminating contrast with the failures of most of their contemporaries. In the early 1840's, our first severe economic depression coincided with a competition in the reprinting of British books. This was so disastrous that it not only bankrupted many American publishers but drove down the retail prices of American books to the point where the literary profession was not self-supporting. When this situation was brought under control in the late 1840's, the profession was ready for Hawthorne the novelist, Emerson the lecturer, and Longfellow the poet.

If I had included a fourth chapter, I would have perhaps devoted it to a problem functionally related to the subjects of the first three: the writer's struggle, in the immature publishing economy of that time, to discover who or what his audience was. C. P. Snow recently stated that "In America [in contrast to England] writers really don't know whom they are writing for." This is an overstatement, of course: it is true only of the kind of writer who is attempting a breakthrough. Thus qualified, the generalization also applies to writers of the 1830's and 1840's, though it needs still further qualification in terms of the regional factors explored in the first chapter, the problems of distribution and of publishing capital alluded to in the second, and the status of literary genres discussed in the third.

Finally, let me confess the limitations imposed on this kind of study by the lack of adequate research tools. Some of my propositions need more statistical support than I have been able to offer. Evans' bibliography of American imprints stops at 1800. For the next two decades (crucial ones for this subject) there is no general catalogue at all. Roorbach's bibliography begins with 1820, but is so incomplete up to 1850 that it is almost worthless for my purposes. Of the bibliographies of literary genres, only Lyle Wright's work on American fiction approaches completeness. Wegelin's list of American poems stops at 1820, and can serve only as a stopgap while we await the publication of the catalogue of the John Carter Brown collection of American poetry at Brown University. The most important unfinished project, however, is the editing and publication of the American Imprints Inventory. Until that is available, we can know little about American editions of foreign works and, therefore, little about the impact of foreign literatures upon our culture.

W. C.

ACKNOWLEDGMENTS

I wish to thank the Guggenheim Foundation, the Huntington Library, the Library of Congress (Grant-in-Aid for Research in American Studies), New York University, and the Ohio State University for providing funds and time for research.

For the use of manuscript materials I am grateful to the libraries of Yale University, Harvard University, and the Historical Society of Pennsylvania; to the New York Public Library and the Huntington Library; and to the Houghton Mifflin Company, Harper and Brothers, and Lea & Febiger.

My colleagues R. D. Altick, R. H. Pearce, C. M. Simpson, and J. H. Wilson made helpful criticisms of the manuscript. Jacob Blanck and Rollo G. Silver have been consistently generous in giving information from their great store of special knowledge about books and publishers.

I owe a special debt of gratitude to Robert E. Spiller; to Kenneth M. Setton, Rudolf Hirsch, and Jesse C. Mills of the Library of the University of Pennsylvania; and to William McCarthy of the Rosenbach Foundation.

CONTENTS

Preface   7

1. Publishing Centers   17

2. Author and Publisher   38

3. Literary Genres and Artifacts   61

Notes   84

Index   91

LITERARY PUBLISHING IN AMERICA
1790-1850

1

PUBLISHING CENTERS

The differences between cities in the Middle West have given rise to a theory that only towns located on navigable water, like Cleveland and Cincinnati, escape the provincialism of landlocked communities, and that cosmopolitanism is possible only when easy accessibility encourages a flow of population. Modern transportation and mass cultural media are rendering the theory obsolete, but in the past it was in accord with the facts; and it has a direct bearing on the subject of publishing centers in America before 1850.

Though railroads were built from 1830 on, water remained the crucial fact in American transportation until mid-century. In the early decades of the century, deep harbor water was a major determinant in the growth of publishing centers, not only because the ocean was the chief highway between our largest towns but because it made a considerable difference in a publisher's prosperity whether the first copy of a new work by Byron or Scott was taken off a boat in his city or some other. Let me anticipate a little at this point by saying that the competition for the reprinting of British literature, harmful to the American writer as it was for a while, helped to bring American literary publishing to maturity: it was the most successful of the early reprint competitors who developed into the most able publishers of American literary works.

But deep harbor water in itself was not enough. Other factors ultimately determined which of the seaports were to control foreign and domestic trade, and decisive among these factors was the river which flowed —or did not flow—into a seaport from the interior. It was, indeed, the conditions of early river transportation which brought about our present custom of publishing important trade books in the autumn and in the spring, for ordinarily the rivers were frozen by December or early January and could not be depended upon again for the shipping of books until March. Publishers' correspondence, from the beginning until the mid-forties, is full of references to the "closing and opening of the navigation." Carey & Lea reported to Cooper in January of 1832 that the unusually early freezing of the rivers (by December 1) had hurt the sale of *The Bravo* because they had not been able to send it to "half the interior towns."[1] A Harper contract book records, as of March 17, 1843, that Theodore Sedgwick Fay's novel, *Hoboken*, was to be issued "so soon as the navigation opens."[2] And as late as 1845, when much railroad transportation was available, a Harper author could write, in mid-November that, "The publishing Season is now nearly closed, [and as soon as] the rivers are frozen . . . it will be over."[3] Since coastal transportration rarely stopped, no matter what the weather, such statements are evidence that eastern publishing customs were to some extent determined by trade with the interior.

Thus it was that publishing interests were deeply involved in the cities' struggle for control of rivers and canals along the Atlantic coast. New York's Harper and Brothers' ultimate victory over Philadelphia's Carey dynasty was foretold in a note in a Columbus, Ohio, newspaper in 1826: "It takes thirty days to transport goods from Philadelphia, and costs $5 per hundred. From New York City to this place, twenty days and costs half."[4] To understand how the Hudson River and Erie Canal system gave New York publishers a crucial head-start in the Ohio trade, one must go to R. G. Albion's magnificent study of early transportation in *The Port of New York*.[5] Similarly, to understand the decline of Baltimore as a publishing center after a promising start, one must read of its losing battle with Philadelphia for control of the Susquehanna, as described by J. W. Livingood.[6] Certainly, Boston's long delayed leadership in literary publishing, even within the borders of New England, is to be explained in part by the fact that no important river flows into its port.

History is full of "ifs" and "might-have-beens," and one that particularly invites reflection is that Hartford, whose literary publishing up to 1830 was as important as Boston's, might have become New England's literary center. One notes with surprise that in 1813, the very year when stereotype printing was introduced in America, a stereotype company was incorporated in Hartford with a capital of $500,000 (an almost incredible figure, considering the notorious undercapitalization of the publishing and printing business at that time), and that two years later another such company was incorporated in that city with a capital of $150,000.[7] But

Hartford could not tap the trade of upper New England because its Connecticut River was almost unnavigable above the Massachusetts border, and nearby New York overwhelmingly dominated the river trade up to Middletown.[8] Certainly the valley was accessible to the New York ships which were carrying Hocquet Caritat's huge circulating fiction libraries to the interior;[9] certainly, also, New York publishers could exploit the book market in western New England more cheaply than could Boston houses.

Rivers, then, must enter into a definition of that slippery phrase, "literary center." For our purposes, it cannot be defined as a place where writers live. At that moment in 1826 when Carey & Lea were becoming the undisputed leaders in American fiction publishing, they wrote James Fenimore Cooper that Philadelphia did everything better in literary affairs—except produce novelists.[10] Our conception of the literary center has been corrupted by a tendency, continuous from Joseph Dennie in the eighteenth century to Van Wyck Brooks in the twentieth, to think of cultural centers in European terms which are not wholly applicable to American facts. Implicit in such thinking is the Greek conception of the metropolis—literally, the mother city, the place in which art and thought are generated, and from which cultural influence flows to the sterile provinces. Hence the early eagerness to identify Philadelphia as the "Athens" of America, or Cincinnati as the "Athens" of the West. Hence, Ezra Pound's ignorant statement that "all great art is born of the metropolis." Hence also Brooks's Spenglerian talk about Boston the "culture city." Richard Shryock long ago pointed out that "Boston once excelled in cultural achievement by the simple device of defining culture in terms of those things in which Boston once excelled."[11] We have also been misled by false analogies between our cities and London, which has always done ninety-nine per cent of literary publishing for the whole of England and in which most English writers have actually lived. Back in 1800, Joseph Dennie yearned for the protection of London's court, and Philip Freneau, lonely and neglected in New York, brooded about "Thrice happy Dryden" who, in London, could "meet some rival bard on every street."

But the relation of the big city to the province and of the writer to society has never been the same in America as in Europe, and one difference has been that our authors have, on the whole, been as alienated from each other as from the rest of society. When they are young they do tend to congregate, and to lean on each other for support, as the Beat Generation are doing now in San Francisco's Co-Existence Bagel Shop; as Cooper's group did in the back room of Wiley's bookstore in New York; or as the Transcendentalists did at Brook Farm. But such groupings have always been ephemeral; when our writers grow up they normally wish only to get away from each other. The idea of their solidarity or propinquity has been sponsored by those literary historians who have tried to reduce the enormous complexity of our literary culture to simple patterns of biographical and geographical relationships, with the result that we tend to think, historically, in terms of isolated groups like the Brahmins, the Connecticut Wits, the Knickerbockers, etc., instead of in terms of the relation of literature to the culture of the country as a whole. Still worse, the biographical method encourages a conception of literature as a one-directional phenomenon—from the writer to the reader, with the implication that the reader is merely passive and receptive, just as the province is supposed to have a merely passive relation with the metropolis.

But in America the provinces have always had a vital and active influence on the culture of cities, and the general reader, or the common reader (he who stands somewhere between the avant garde and the consumers of mass diversion), has had a greater and more direct influence on the writer than his counterpart in Europe has had. This statement can be documented conclusively from internal evidence in the work of our greatest writers.

Reciprocity between writer and reader, then, has been of the essence in our literary history, and it is this which leads me to define the American cultural center as the place or places in which reciprocal influences are explicitly and crucially operative; where the publisher not only accepts or rejects but influences literary work through his knowledge of taste in the country as a whole; and where changes in public taste are often initiated through a publisher's willingness to let a writer open up new literary territory.

Let us grant that mutations in public taste are slow and infrequent—that the common reader's appetite is for the derivative writer and the competent craftsman —for the Irvings, the Bryants, the Coopers, the Longfellows, the J. P. Marquands, and the James Gould Cozzens's—not for the (to use Robert Spiller's phrase) "original and organic" artist, who, much as he may be "the most profound expression" of his time, does not represent the taste of his time. Not a single literary work of genuine originality published in book form before 1850 had any commercial value to speak of until much later, and most of our classics were financial failures—Poe's and Hawthorne's tales, Emerson's essays and poems, Melville's *Mardi*, Thoreau's *Week*. This study must then be primarily concerned with that middle brow, middle range of literature, serious but not necessarily original, which is, and always has been, the bread and butter of respectable publishers.

I identify as publishing centers during the first half of the nineteenth century those cities in which publishers, seeking the trade not only of the coast but of the interior, discovered (in a sense, established) the common denominators in the literary taste of the whole country. These cities were Philadelphia and New York, which, close together and connected by abundant ocean, river,[12] and road transportation, formed what I shall call the publishing axis. In general, Philadelphia publishers controlled the southern book-buying market, and New York the territory west of the Hudson, both cities sharing the trade of the Ohio Valley. As the century advanced, readers in these areas, whose culture was turning into something different from that of the coastal urban centers, exerted more and more influence on what was published in the axis. When, after 1850, railroads enabled Boston to mitigate its geographical isolation, the interior began to influence Boston publishing in a way that it had not done when New England was publishing chiefly for itself.

This influence of the interior on the coast has, I think, some bearing on Mr. Spiller's theory of the cycle of American literature,[13] which I restate and adapt to my own purposes as follows: The literary forms and thought of Europe, after a period of acculturation on our Atlantic Coast, were transmitted to the interior by magazine and book publishers in the axis, whose policies were influenced by the taste of the hinterland.

For specific examples of this cycle in operation, we observe that the misery novel of the *Charlotte Temple* type, which was reduced to popular formula in London by the lady writers[14] of the Minerva Press in the 1790's, was reprinted by Carey in Philadelphia, and distributed through his outlets in Pennsylvania and the South (by Parson Weems, among others). Having thus exploited the public appetite for diverting fiction, Carey was ready to take the lead in reprinting Scott two decades later. When Cooper took up the historical novel in the twenties Carey was able to get him away from New York rivals partly because, through reprints of Scott, he had developed the biggest fiction market in the country and could estimate pretty accurately how many copies of a novel he could sell. When Cooper became popular in Europe, and was actually imitated in such works as Dumas' *Les Mohicans de Paris,* the cycle was complete—the historical novel, born in the Old World, had been imported by the axis, acculturated by Cooper, popularized in the interior by Carey, and returned to the Old World.

The magazine world offers a different kind of example. George Graham of Philadelphia, whose magazine was one of the first to hit a common denominator of

taste throughout the whole country, explained to Longfellow in 1844 why he would not pay Lowell top prices
for his verse: "I have done a good deal . . . for Lowell's
reputation . . . but I know the test of *general* popularity
as well as any man—and he has it not. He is well known
in New England and appreciated there but has not a
tythe of the reputation *South and West* possessed by
yourself and Bryant. This of course I *know*—it is no
guess work, for with a thousand exchange papers scattered all over the whole Union I should be a dolt in
business not to see who is most copied and praised
by them."[15]

Observe that all three of the poets mentioned were
receivers and adapters of European culture, and had
developed reputations on the coast; but that when
western and southern editors selected Graham material
for reprinting, they tended to reject Lowell. Noting
this fact, Graham tended to reject Lowell too, so that
we find the taste of the West determining, to some
extent, the literary fare offered to readers in the East.
And Graham's judgment was correct: Throughout the
country as a whole, Lowell remained the least popular
of the Brahmins.

Statistics on regional imprints are still entirely inadequate, but one can, tentatively, at least, lay out a
general pattern of the development of publishing centers, as follows:

(1) Up to about 1820 literary publishing was local
and decentralized—except in the Philadelphia area. A
writer published where he happened to live, and if he
happened to live, say, in Walpole, New Hampshire, as
did Royall Tyler, his work had little circulation. As

Joseph Dennie wrote of Tyler's *The Algerine Captive* in 1797, "It is . . . extremely difficult for the Bostonians to supply themselves with a book that slumbers in a stall at Walpole. . . ."[16]

(2) If a writer was determined to get the widest possible distribution (as was true of Connecticut's Joel Barlow when he was ready to publish the *Columbiad* in 1807), and if he could afford to finance the work himself, he took his book to New York or Philadelphia —preferably to Philadelphia, and most likely to Mathew Carey.

(3) In the New York-Philadelphia axis, literary traffic—and writers—moved briskly, in both directions. A number of publishers had offices in both towns, and almost all of them had agents in the other.

(4) Because of the dominating geographical position of the axis, the process of centralization proceeded most rapidly in this region.

(5) The strongest evidence of centralization is in the field of fiction, the most lucrative of literary genres. In the first decade of the nineteenth century, almost fifty per cent of our native fiction was published outside of New York, Boston, and Philadelphia—in the 1840's, only eight per cent. But the great majority of the standard two-volume novels which are respectfully mentioned in literary histories were published in New York and Philadelphia.

(6) In the forties, Philadelphia began to lose its control of the book trade in the South and West, and supremacy in literary publishing moved toward New York; specifically, it moved away from the Carey-Lea-Blanchard firms, which had done the most important

literary publishing in the country, to the Harpers. Whereas in the thirties the Carey-Leas had published one hundred and forty-two fiction titles to Harpers' ninety-one, in the forties the Harpers forged ahead with ninety-six to the Philadelphia firm's eighty-six.

(7) Until the 1830's, New England publishing remained decentralized, and Boston lagged far behind New York and Philadelphia in its development as a national literary center. As a result, much of the famous New England flowering before 1850 took place, as far as publishing was concerned, in New York and Philadelphia. Among those who took their works to publishers and editors in these cities were Hawthorne, Whittier, Prescott, Longfellow, and Lowell; and it is safe to say that Emerson's influence was restricted and delayed because he did all his publishing in Boston. It would, I think, be easy to demonstrate that Boston publishers did not even know they had a renaissance on their hands until Ticknor & Fields woke up in the late forties.

An important aspect of the situation in Boston was the provincialism of that city. One of the commonly accepted indices of cosmopolitanism is a city's support of an active theater. If we turn to Arthur Hobson Quinn's list of first productions of American plays,[17] we learn that Boston's share in such risks steadily declined from the eighteenth century, when it had eleven new productions, compared to Philadelphia's sixteen and New York's thirty-three, down to the 1830's, when it produced only eleven compared to Philadelphia's forty-nine and New York's sixty-five.

But let us listen to the writers themselves. We hear

a good deal about New England authors who lived in or near Boston, but little about the many who left it or avoided it. When Joel Barlow contemplated a career in the book business in 1784, his first thoughts were of Hartford and Baltimore, not Boston. We need not take too seriously Joseph Dennie's bitter valedictory to that city—that "Jewish, peddling, and commercial quarter," but we listen with interest when he says that in Philadelphia, where he made a success of America's first important literary magazine, society respected him "as a professed man of letters."[18]

And things got worse in Boston rather than better. Edward Everett, comparing Boston unfavorably with Baltimore in 1820, said that in his town "it is scarcely possible to say anything which will not bring you into personal collision with your acquaintances."[19] Catharine Sedgwick of the Berkshires, all of whose most successful books were published in the axis, said, as she breathed the free air of Philadelphia during a visit in 1830, that the Bostonians "were afraid to speak lest they commit themselves for life."[20] Even the circumspect Longfellow, sick of Boston's perpetual sniping at Harvard, Channing, and the abolitionists, wrote in 1837 that this "Little-Peddlington community" was only a "great village. The tyranny of public opinion there surpasses all belief."[21] This was the decade and the place of which Van Wyck Brooks says "there was a springtime feeling in the air"; but he does not quote young professional writers like N.P. Willis and Park Benjamin who fled the town in the thirties, Willis saying, "They have denied me patronage, abused me, misrepresented me, refused me both character and genius.

. . . The mines of Golconda would not tempt me to return and live in Boston."[22] This was also the time when Boston's liveliest general literary magazines moved to New York because they had not been able to get sufficient circulation in New England to support them.

I think we must recognize the fact that until mid-century, when Ticknor & Fields were fully committed to making a specialty of belles-lettres, the New England publishing economy was unable to support its literary renaissance. Two letters of the mid-forties suggest the reason why. In 1845 Nathaniel Hawthorne, having published his first nine books in Boston without success, took two books to publishers in New York (where he was already sending most of his magazine contributions), and tried to persuade Emerson to do likewise. "His reputation," wrote Hawthorne to a publisher's advisor, "is still, I think, provincial, and almost local partly owing to the defects of the New England system of publication."[23] A year later Emerson indirectly confirmed the judgment. Having refused a New York offer for his collected poems, he admitted that a Boston publisher would not exert himself to get a wide circulation for the work because "he will prefer to sell at his own counter and monopolize the retail commission, which is larger." But, he added with characteristic naïveté about the book world, "If the book is good, the distant trader will have to send for it. . . ."[24] One can imagine the eagerness with which a Cincinnati bookseller would send for a stock of Transcendentalist poetry, especially considering Emerson's conviction that a discount of one-fifth or one-sixth was an adequate inducement at a time when one-third was becoming standard.

If Emerson looks like a special case because of his lack of popular appeal, consider that Lydia Huntley Sigourney of Hartford, whose publisher (James Munroe) was also Emerson's, complained that her books were unavailable not only in Ohio but in *Hartford*.[25]

The basic facts seem to be, then, that most New England publishers were primarily retailers with little interest in the wholesaling which major publishers in the axis emphasized; that they therefore tended to publish for their immediate neighborhood; and that they tried to monopolize the retail sale of their publications in their own cities. This would seem to be an incredible publishing practice unless one recognizes that New England had the most extraordinarily concentrated book-buying and reading public in the whole country, and that from the mid-eighteenth century its publishers had been able and content to survive on the basis of local consumption of their wares. Consider that among the imprints of Thomas Collier, an eighteenth century publisher in the isolated western Connecticut mountain village of Litchfield, were a two-volume translation of Goethe's *The Sorrows of Young Werther*, reprints of British novels like Mackenzie's *Man of Feeling* and of the poetry of Pope, Goldsmith, and Gray, and a 1793 anthology of American poetry[26]. Since other New England Village publishers had similar lists, it would seem that they printed small editions of general literary works for a local audience. In this respect New England was strikingly different from other regions. Not only did Philadelphia and New York control the outlets in the South and West; they did the publishing for those areas, whereas Boston competed with publishers in scores of New England small towns.

The earliest example for which I can give reasonably complete figures is Tom Paine's *Common Sense* (1776), of which forty-six editions were published in the eighteenth century.[27] In the area controlled by Philadelphia, that city published fifteen out of seventeen editions; though Virginia absorbed as many as a thousand copies at a time, not a single edition was published in the whole of the South. In the New York area, one edition was published in Albany, all other editions (three) in New York City. But in New England, of twenty-three editions, Boston published only two, nine other towns a total of twenty-one, and seven of these towns published as many as, or more than, Boston. Of all American editions, New England published exactly one-half; but Boston was obviously not its publishing center, for Providence and Newport each printed twice as many editions as Boston.

Lest this be interpreted as a freak of politics or patriotism, look at the figures for eighteenth-century reprints of certain British classics. Of editions of Samuel Richardson's novels, all nine in the Philadelphia area were published in Philadelphia; but in New England, Boston published a total of five, and four other towns a total of six. Of editions of *Robinson Crusoe*, Philadelphia published six of the eight editions in its area, and New York City, all five editions in its area; but of New England's eleven editions, Boston published only four, and six other towns published seven.[28]

The figures for another foreign novel, Mrs. Rowson's

Charlotte Temple,[29] from its first reprinting in 1794 to 1840, are probably nearly complete. In the Philadelphia area, five towns published twenty-one editions, Philadelphia issuing fourteen of these. New York State published eighteen, fourteen of them in New York City. But of twenty-nine New England editions, only two were issued in Boston (compared to Hartford's thirteen), whereas eight other towns published a total of twenty-seven.

We also have probably complete figures for the period 1790-1829 for one of the most popular of eighteenth-century poems, Pope's *Essay on Man.*[30] The usual pattern prevailed in the Philadelphia and New York areas, but in New England it was even more pronounced. That region published a total of seventy-seven editions —three times as many as all the rest of the country put together. But of these seventy-seven, Boston published only nine, whereas thirty-four other towns, in all six New England states, published a total of sixty-eight. Can there be any doubt that Windsor, Vermont's six editions—or Boston's nine—were printed for anything but local consumption?

But perhaps the *Essay on Man* is a special case, for many of the village editions might have been printed for the local schools or academies for which New England was famous. Let us look at the figures for highly mixed types of publication. We have records of all works, literary and otherwise, copyrighted and printed in the two states of Massachusetts and Virginia during the decade 1800 to 1809.[31] Since the titles include all state laws and legal documents, which were usually published in the state capital, one might expect a

radically different pattern, but not so. Virginia, older
than Massachusetts, published a total of only fourteen
titles in ten years, eleven of them in Richmond and a
total of three in three other towns. In Massachusetts
the total was 303 titles. The capital published fifty-four
per cent, and twenty-one other towns in the state published all the rest. Incidentally, it is some evidence of
New England's extraordinary literacy that in this early
decade, Massachusetts actually published ten times as
many titles as it copyrighted—a total of 3,430.

The test of our literary centers must ultimately be
in terms of the publication of American literature, but
here we get into statistical difficulties. I eliminate
printed drama because it is and always has been a
highly specialized publishing product, and I pause here
only to note that New York, which printed forty-five
per cent of all plays to 1830, was indisputably the center of this activity.[32]

Poetry publishing will be impossible to get at statisti-
cally until more bibliographical work has been done on
it. But in any case, I doubt the value of a statistical
approach to the subject. The historian can support
Robert Graves's recent statement that "poetry is an
embarrassing subject in the publishing trade and does
not lend itself to statistics."[33] Longfellow and Whittier
notwithstanding, poetry is and always has been primarily an avocation—an amateur activity rather than
a professional one. One would judge by Wegelin's list
that in the years, 1800 to 1820, half of all verse was
published outside the three literary centers, and one
suspects that most of it was issued by the local printer,
in pamphlet form, at the author's expense. Even when

we get more complete lists, it may still be difficult to tell how many titles were in this category, but Kindilien's study of American poetry in the eighteen nineties[34] leads one to believe that verse continued to be, for the most part, something that was not marketed but inflicted on friends and libraries.

Nevertheless, we can chart the rise of professional poetry, from its inauspicious beginning in William Cullen Bryant's 1821 volume.[35] That he had it printed in Cambridge and published in Boston was prophetic, for Cambridge skill in poetry printing was to lead to a country-wide conviction within the next thirty years, that in no other place could printers set up a page of poetry properly, and that only in Boston could poetry be published with adequate dignity and prestige. Even when New England poets like Longfellow and Lowell published in New York, they preferred to have their stereotype plates made in Cambridge.

But in 1821 Bryant had to take the entire financial risk on his volume, pay a commission to the publisher for handling it, and allow bookstores to take it on consignment. Characteristically, his publisher monopolized the retail sale in Boston, where it was available in only two other stores. Of the edition of 750 copies, retailing at 37½ cents, only 270 were disposed of in two years.

Clearly, Bryant's Boston publisher did not make him a nationally known poet; for that ultimate event, New York and Philadelphia were responsible. His professional poetic career did not begin until the Harpers, with their tremendous market in the West, brought out a series, at their own risk, of at least ten editions from 1836 to 1846, paying him a royalty of twenty-five cents a copy. After *Graham's Magazine* discovered, and helped to establish, his universal appeal, Carey & Hart of Philadelphia secured the book rights, and in the late forties sold 1700 copies a year in two different formats, paying Bryant over $1500 in three years.[36] The country was now ready to absorb the almost yearly editions issued by Appleton of New York to the end of the century.

It was the publishers of the axis, then, that made Bryant a national poet. More than that, it can be argued that Philadelphia did much to make possible Ticknor & Field's achievement in poetry publishing. By the middle forties, Carey & Hart, and H. C. Baird were making a specialty of expensive, illustrated editions not only of Bryant, but of Longfellow, Willis, and others, to say nothing of their immensely influential editions of Griswold's *Poets and Poetry of America*. Issuing such works at prices ranging up to $7.50 for illustrated editions, these publishers helped to give American verse a luxury status it had never had before. This was not a wholly fortunate circumstance, since it encouraged the common reader to think of verse as an appendage to sentimental pictures, but such cultural damage had begun back in the 1820's, when Philadelphia produced the first illustrated annual giftbooks.

Rare as true professionalism is in poetry, it has been the norm in the novel since the time of Cooper. Vanity publishing of novels is unusual, simply because it costs so much, and although, before Cooper, many amateurs made an attempt or two, thereafter the centralization and commercialization of fiction proceeded with great rapidity, especially in the axis. True to pattern, the process was slowest in New England, where, up to 1830, forty-four per cent of all fiction titles were published outside of Boston in a total of sixty-two towns; but by the forties, Boston's percentage was about the same as that of the axis.[37]

There is one curious thing in Boston's fiction record. On the one hand, it is hard to think of a single, respectable, professional novelist who published regularly in Boston before 1850. On the other hand, by the 1840's that city was publishing almost as much fiction, in sheer quantity, as New York and much more than Philadelphia. This was because it had become a center for the publishing of cheap mass fiction, like Lucius Manlius Sargent's temperance tales, often brief and usually unbound, which were printed by the hundreds of thousands. At mid-century, then, Boston was distinguished for its publishing at the top and at the bottom of the literary scale—for its poetry, history, and philosophy, and for its fictional trash.

It is a temptation to conclude these remarks with speculations which might provide a new key to the literary history of the period—to postulate, for example, that because the publishers in the axis homogenized, so to speak, the taste of the Middle Coast, the West, and the South, they courted and encouraged the kind of literary mediocrity that would suit such a mixed audience; that they attracted the secondary writers— the Irvings, Bryants, Coopers, Kennedys, Pauldings, Sedgwicks, Willis's, Longfellows; and moreover that they tempted these writers to stay in tried and safe grooves and not to experiment (for this latter there is some evidence in the publishing correspondence of Cooper). One might argue, concomitantly, that Boston published writers of more lasting repute—Emerson, Thoreau, Hawthorne; that because these New Englanders wrote without much hope of profit, for a local audience which they understood, they could attempt new things, take chances, preserve their integrity—in a word, that the very provincialism of New England was their passport to posterity.

Perhaps there is something to it. But the theory leaves out of account the fact that the axis publishers also courted all the great New Englanders, even when there was no evidence that they could be popular. Also, it takes no account of two other artists—Poe and Melville—residents of New York and Philadelphia and therefore not eligible for the benefits of provincialism. Both earnestly worked to attract that national audience to which their publishers had access, and which made the lesser writers relatively prosperous. Both yielded to publishers' pressures and tried to adjust to the national taste. Yet all of Poe's books were commercial failures; and so were all of Melville's books for which he himself had any lasting respect. Both had to wait longer than the New Englanders for America to appreciate their best work, and they did most of their waiting in their graves.

No—such speculations lead to dead ends. Yet my central thesis remains: Up to 1850, the publishers of the axis were the discoverers and interpreters of American literary taste and were the channel through which the taste of the South and West moved, to influence—for better or worse—the production of literature on the coast. And the New England writers had a national hearing precisely to the extent that they went to Philadelphia and New York to get it.

2

AUTHOR AND PUBLISHER

The first era of successful professional authorship in America began in the years 1819 to 1821 with the publication of Irving's *Sketch Book* and James Fenimore Cooper's *The Spy*. The twenty years that followed were notable for a tremendous expansion of the national economy. Except for minor recessions in the late twenties and in 1834 and 1837, which the book trade duly reflected,[1] it was, to use Irving's phrase, a time of "unexampled prosperity." Equally unexampled in the history of the profession were Irving's income of $23,500 in the year 1829—all from books—and Cooper's average of $6,500 a year in the 1820's. No first-rate author of the brilliant fifties—the years of the American renaissance—came even close to such affluence. The reasons are many; for the major ones we must look into the book trade economy and the changes in it between 1820 and 1850.

On December 19, 1819, Mathew Carey of Philadelphia—publisher, bookseller, and chief jobber for the southern states, sent what was probably, in America, a record-breaking order for a purely literary work. It was for four hundred copies of the fifth number of *The Sketch Book*: "Send 150 by Swiftsure Stage and the remainder by Mercantile Line." Number five was a slim pamphlet which sold for what was also probably a record-breaking price—seventy-five cents. The order was the climax of a controversy. It was sent to Ebenezer Irving in New York (Washington was in England) rather than to the printer because the Irvings had paid for the manufacture of *The Sketch Book* and therefore were in complete control of sales and discount policy. Orders for the first American classic had been coming in to Carey from bookstores throughout the South and Middle States, but he had been unwilling to fill them. A Philadelphia rival, Moses Thomas, had had a monopoly on all sales in the area, and Carey had had to pay him sixty-five and one-half cents (a discount of one-sixth) for a book which he himself had to sell to country booksellers for sixty cents. But because Thomas was close to insolvency, Carey had managed to break his monopoly by appealing to C. S. Van Winkle, the New York printer of the work, who interceded with Ebenezer. As a result, Carey was given the usual one-fourth discount, four-fifths of which he gave up on those copies which he sold to his retailers. It was a small profit for a wholesaler, but he had to supply the booksellers' demand, for many of them bought their entire stock of books from him.

Reconstructing the account from such correspondence as survives,[2] one finds that the score on *Sketch Book No. 5* was somewhat as follows:

Printing	26¼ cents	35 per cent
Discount	18¾ "	25 " "
(Retailer 20%		
Wholesaler 5%)		
Profit (for Irving)	30 "	40 " "

The set of seven pamphlets which constituted the work

cost the retail buyer $5.37½—an enormous price in America, where Scott's novels were selling for two dollars. In setting such high prices Irving was following British practice, and that he succeeded in it—just this once—is a not wholly comprehensible historical accident. There were protests (especially in thrifty New England) against the price of *The Sketch Book* and what was then considered its luxurious format, but an estimated five thousand American readers were willing to buy it, and Irving's profit for two years was, incredibly, over nine thousand dollars. But his publishing methods contained the seeds of their own destruction.

The economic history of *The Sketch Book* reveals all the elements of the early American writer's publishing problem: the retail price of books, the cost of manufacture, the discount to the trade, and the division of profit between author and publisher. The basic pattern, which seems to have been borrowed from England, allowed one-third of the retail price for manufacturing costs, one-third for trade discount, and one-third for profit, which theoretically was divided equally between author and publisher. (Note that the author's share of this profit was the equivalent of a sixteen and two-thirds per cent royalty.)

But, from the start, American facts upset the British formula. In the first place, British publishers kept competition under control through "courtesy of the trade" and other more coercive devices; kept retail prices high through collusion, even to the extent of destroying "remainders" rather than dumping them at low prices; had a closely predictable sale for every type of book; and, in general, enjoyed all the advantages of a geographically small and homogeneous market. As a result, they were able to keep retail prices at a high and stable level that was impossible in our primitive American conditions. By 1821, many new British novels (usually issued in three volumes) were selling for thirty-one and a half shillings, or about $7.30 in American money. The same novels sold for two dollars in American reprints. One can see why no American writer could hope to achieve Scott's income (for a period) of ten thousand pounds a year.

In the second place, in the early twenties American publishers were not accustomed to paying anything at all to native writers, nor did they, except on rare, and usually unfortunate occasions, print native literary works at their own risk. Hence, when Irving and Cooper found that they could produce literature of commercial value, they followed the established custom and financed their own works; and because they held the purse strings they decreed the discounts that were to be allowed. There was, of course, no obligation to divide profits equally with the so-called publisher, who simply acted as wholesale distributor. As a result, what we think of as the normal arrangement between author and publisher was often reversed: instead of being paid royalties by publishers, authors, in effect, paid publishers a royalty. The publisher got his pay either in the form of a commission which he charged for distributing the work, or from the difference between the whole discount he was allowed—say, one-third—and the smaller discount which he allowed the retailer.

But though the author could, under these conditions, make a profit of forty per cent or more, the system worked against him in some ways. When a publisher reprinted a foreign work at his own risk, he divided what would have been the author's profit with his retailers in the form of high discounts, which encouraged the retailers to push sales. But the small discount which the retailer received on a copyrighted native work was no inducement to salesmanship. Hence American books had a relatively smaller circulation than foreign ones partly because the retailer had smaller incentive to sell them. Even when the publishing economy became more mature, the retailer's natural prejudice against native works continued. As late as 1848, Ticknor & Fields wrote a Cincinnati dealer that their discount on a certain list was one-third—except for Longfellow's works, which discounted at twenty-five to twenty-eight per cent because "the copyright [we pay] is unusually high." The same firm offered only twenty-five per cent on *The Scarlet Letter*.[3]

The difficulties of early American authorship are often attributed to American prejudice against American literature. But equally important was the lack of adequate risk capital in the publishing industry. Its members lived on such a narrow margin that not many had a life of more than a few years. Carey's was the only eighteenth century firm that lived on long into the nineteenth (its capital of a quarter of a million dollars in 1834 was uniquely high),[4] and of those firms established before 1820, only the Harpers prospered beyond mid-century. The panic of 1837 was particularly disastrous, but even the slightest recession brought on a rash of bankruptcies, reorganizations, or assignments of assets. Few authors escaped losses in one or more of these failures.

This lack of capital resulted in a number of different arrangements by which the writer took the whole or some of the risk of publication, sometimes to his own advantage, sometimes to the advantage of the publisher. He took the entire risk when he paid the cost of manufacture, paid a commission to a distributor, and allowed the retailer to receive the work on consignment. This was the normal fate of the untried author, like Bryant with his early poems, and R. H. Dana, Sr., with *The Idle Man* (one of several attempts to emulate Irving's success with *The Sketch Book*).

A safer variation of this method was that of Irving and Cooper before they took their business to Carey. These two paid for manufacture, but sold whole editions to jobbers who took the risk of unsold copies.

Still better was the method adopted by Prescott and other historians in the thirties, and Longfellow and Lowell in the forties. Here the author paid only for the stereotype plates and retained ownership. Sometimes he leased them to a publisher for a stated period, but normally he was paid a relatively high royalty, at the time of issue, for each edition printed from his plates. The difference between the normal ten per cent and Longfellow's twenty per cent gave him a high return for his investment in plates, because his works were often reprinted.

Seemingly fair, but frequently pernicious, was the half-profits system. The publisher made no payments until his risk of manufacturing costs was covered, and he often yielded to the temptation of padding the actual costs of production, or added a commission charge for his services. This was the Harpers' favorite method with novelists in the 1830's,[5] and Herman Melville was its victim for over thirty years. He owned the plates of his first book, *Typee*, but for all others he was on the half-profits system; and on *Pierre*, the publisher actually exempted the first 1190 copies from royalty. Moreover, Melville always borrowed in advance against a new book, and was charged interest for these advances, so that he was in debt to the Harpers for almost his entire career.[6]

At the other extreme was an arrangement which few authors but Irving and Cooper could make, and they only with the house of Carey. Carey purchased the right to publish their works for a term of years, for a stated sum; they took no risk and made no investment themselves, and were paid whether a work sold or not. Even in modern times there is no equivalent to this arrangement, except when really large advances are made against future royalties. In originating this system, Carey anticipated the later arrangement (which was carried over into the twentieth century) whereby established authors got contracts and payments for works before they were completed or even written.

This variety of ways of sharing or assuming the risks of publication resulted in professional fortunes that ranged from feast to famine, depending upon whether a writer had no capital, like Poe, Hawthorne, and Melville, or enough to dictate terms to his publisher, like Cooper, Irving, Longfellow, and Prescott.

Many changes in publishing conditions took place

between 1820 and 1850. At the time of *The Sketch Book*, relations between retailers, printers, publishers, and jobbers were extremely complex. Almost all publishers were retailers; many printers were also publishers and sometimes also retailers; all jobbers were retailers; no jobber could deal profitably in the books of all publishers; and no publisher could reach directly all markets in the country. Currency and credit were so unstable that the mere process of paying and getting paid was difficult. The result was a system of distribution so complicated that the publishers were almost as confused as the historian who tries to read their surviving records and correspondence. It is no wonder that when Richardson & Lord of Boston formed a partnership in 1820, their articles of agreement stated their intention of engaging in the "art, trade, and mystery of bookselling."[7]

The basis of the system was a loose inter-city structure of tie-ins between particular booksellers. A large publisher had agreements with one or more firms in every other large city. These firms were called "correspondents" and acted as bankers, post office, retailers, co-publishers, and sometimes jobbers for their principals. The correspondent was a co-publisher when he co-operated in the issue of a book under the multiple-imprint system, whereby a firm split the risk on a book which it had contracted to distribute. Suppose, as in the case of *Sketch Book No. 1*, a first edition of two thousand copies was published simultaneously in four cities—New York, Philadelphia, Boston, and Baltimore. The printer and quasi-publisher, C. S. Van Winkle of New York, arranged with his correspondents in the other three cities to take, say, five hundred copies each, at a twenty-five per cent discount, the names of all four firms appearing on the cover as a multiple-imprint. Each of the correspondents took charge of publicity for the work in his region. Probably no returns of unsold copies were allowed: the correspondents shared the risk with Van Winkle. But their risk was mitigated by their regional monopoly: no copy could be bought in New England, for example, except from the Boston correspondent, who split his discount with the retailers who bought from him.

If the work was a book rather than a pamphlet, the publishers usually sent sheets (or folded "gatherings") to his correspondents, who had them bound up locally. This fact explains why so many first editions of the time survive in a number of different bindings. Somewhat later, it happened occasionally that a publisher ordered one or more extra sets of stereotype plates. He would sell a set of these to a bookseller, say in Cincinnati, who would print a new title page bearing his own imprint and that of the original publisher. This, again, was a way of dividing risk, for extra sets of plates, inexpensively cast from the same forms as the first set, were sold at a considerable profit, or were paid for by a charge for each copy printed therefrom.

The multiple imprint system was probably at its peak in 1820; certainly so far as literary works were concerned, it was on the decline from then on. By 1850, most publishers had enough capital to manufacture their books at their own risk; and distribution had so improved, with the spread of railroads, that many booksellers in the interior did their buying directly from publishers.

Necessary in its time, the multiple imprint system was doomed. Its vices were regional monopoly and an unprofitable division of discounts. A potential purchaser in Boston might know, through advertisements, that *The Sketch Book* was available in the correspondent's shop, but if he lived on the other side of the town he might not bother to make the trip. The Boston correspondent was willing to supply the work to, and split his discount with, a bookseller in Salem; but in Boston he was likely to prefer to monopolize the retail sale and keep the whole discount himself—if he was sure his whole stock would sell. This practice was fine for the correspondent, but bad for the purchaser—and for the author.

The same objections applied to the "exchange" system. Periodically, the publisher printed a list of his publications, sent it to his correspondents in other cities, and received their lists in return. Each ordered from the other as many books as he could use. No cash changed hands until the end of the year, when the books were balanced and the debtor paid the creditor. In 1822, Carey's correspondent in New York was Wiley & Halstead; in Boston, Wells & Lilly. Apparently (the facts are not entirely clear) in Philadelphia, some of Wiley's titles could be bought only at Carey's; and in New York, some of Carey's only at Wiley's. However, the larger publishers sold some books—especially the less popular or the more doubtful ones—to non-correspondents as well. These were either purchased outright on credit, or taken "on sale" or "commission," the retailer returning unsold copies at the end of a stated period. About the latter, there was constant bickering because sometimes, for example, a Boston book, sent to Louisville on commission, was returned at the end of the year in shopworn condition, when the popularity of the work had passed.

For a period in the early twenties, New York and Philadelphia publishers competed through their correspondents for the first sales of new books in the smaller towns of New York, Pennsylvania, and New Jersey. Carey complained bitterly about a clever co-operative move among New York booksellers to corner the small-town market for themselves. When one of the New York firms published a new and popular British novel, it divided up the whole edition among half-a-dozen of the booksellers of the city. All the firms then supplied the correspondents in Pennsylvania and other smaller towns before they sold in quantity to a large Philadelphia jobber like Carey. When Carey tried to buy a large quantity at a big discount, he was forced to take small lots from six New York firms at small discounts. "It is the case with almost every book published in New York for a considerable time," he wrote Wiley & Halstead in 1820.[8] The result was that he was squeezed from two directions: he could not get a discount large enough to make jobbing profitable, and he found some small towns supplied before he could get to them.

Such schemes were profitable for the New Yorkers, but they were not good for the trade. Even the allotment of territories to specific booksellers operated unfairly. Ebenezer Irving gave the Charleston rights to *The Sketch Book* to a bookseller named Mills, and refused Carey's order to ship a number of copies direct to his own correspondent in Charleston. Thus Carey, a legitimate jobber, with correspondents who depended on him, was unable to supply them with a popular work.

Obviously the methods of book distribution were inadequate; and certainly publishing did not mix well with jobbing and retailing. The most prosperous, stable, and long-lived publishing houses avoided the confusion. Carey gave up his retail business in 1830, and probably his jobbing for other publishers at the same time. One reason why his rich and powerful neighbor to the north, the house of Harper, became the oldest general publisher in America was that, from its founding in 1817, it restricted itself to printing and publishing.

Discounts were at the core of the American writer's problem. In 1820, in both England and America, the average discount to the trade was one-third, though the range was from twenty-five per cent to forty per cent—even fifty per cent, depending on quantity. These rates, however, applied only to books on which little or no royalty was paid. In the twenties, works for which American writers were paid rarely discounted for more than twenty-five per cent, many for less. In 1821-22, twenty-five per cent was the regular discount for Irving's *Sketch Book*, and Cooper's *The Spy*. Two documents from the beginning and end of the twenties show what this situation meant in the competition. On May 5, 1820, Moses Thomas wrote Carey, "I will take 50 [Scott's] *Monastery* at 40pc. and pay for them in Salmagundi [Paulding's second series] at 25pc. The terms on which I get the *Sketch Book* are such that I cannot include that."[9] (On the *Sketch Book* he offered only one-sixth.) In 1829, Carey printed a list of his prices to the trade: Scott's, Disraeli's, and Moore's works were discounted at from fifty per cent to sixty-six and two-thirds per cent. Cooper's oldest works were offered at fifty per cent, a later one at forty per cent, and two new ones at twenty-five per cent. In Boston the situation was even worse. A twenty per cent discount on American works was common, and in the early forties Emerson decreed discounts as small as ten per cent on some of his books.

In the years when Irving and Cooper showed that a literary profession in America was possible, the publishing industry was unprepared for it. The popularity of *The Sketch Book* and *The Spy* made the more alert firms lift their heads and sniff the wind for commercially desirable literary works. Venturesome small fry like Van Winkle, and Wiley & Halstead in New York, were literary-minded and popular with authors, but they lacked capital, and their business methods were often slovenly. Year after year, publishing firms went out of business, or formed new combinations and died again—unable to keep up with the bewildering changes in the American economy. In 1815, when Bradford & Inskeep, the Philadelphia publishers of *The History of New York*, went bankrupt, dragging Moses Thomas down with them, Irving wrote that Thomas was "not to be censured in the affair otherwise than for having conducted his business in the same diffuse, sprawling manner in which all our principal booksellers dash forward into difficulty. . . . These failures I am afraid will sensibly affect the interests of literature and deter all those from the exercise of the pen who would take it up as a means of profit."[10] Some publishers grew stronger as time went by, but twenty-four years later, Samuel Ward, reporting to Longfellow on the unreliability of Samuel Colman of New York, made a typical judgment: "The whole race of booksellers among us are a pack of inefficient felons. With little means and, if possible, less credit, they undertake what they fail to perform."[11]

It is no wonder, then, that in the early twenties our successful authors used publishers only as agents and directed the business of manufacture and distribution themselves in order to protect their profits. Perhaps it was fortunate for Cooper that when he approached Wiley concerning the publication of *The Spy* the latter could offer to serve only as middleman. In 1821, Cooper paid the bills for the first volume of *The Spy* directly to the printer, and, when the whole was published on December 21, Wiley instructed his correspondents that the author was not only the sole owner of the work but was dictating the discounts.[12]

How many copies of this famous first edition (it is now rarer than Poe's *Tamerlane*) were printed can only be guessed at. Two weeks after publication, six hundred had been sold, and these were going in lots of fifty and a hundred. The first edition was probably one thousand, the second fifteen hundred, and the third two thousand—a total of forty-five hundred. At an average profit of forty-five cents, or twenty-two and one-half per cent, Cooper's receipts for the three editions must have been over $2,000.[13] The American novel as an economic fact and an important social institution now came into being. On the other hand, if Cooper had received one-half the profits of an equal sale in England, at a guinea a copy, he would have earned almost double the amount.

American authors must have been inspired by the success of *The Spy*, for the number of novels produced in this decade was more than triple that of the preceding. But the sale was not so good as it might have been, and the records of Carey & Lea show why. When Wiley wrote Carey about *The Spy*, the latter, long a sponsor of native writers, answered, "Send your book without delay."[14] When Carey had read the book, five days after publication, he wrote, "We will take 100 *Spy* on the terms proposed in order to do what we can to encourage American literature.[15] But his orders for a total of seven hundred and fifty copies were accompanied by complaints. Buying the book in sheets, to be bound in Philadelphia, he found signatures missing. The term of credit was too short: he bought at three-to-four months and had to sell at six-to-twelve months. Above all, the discount was too small. At one-third it was more generous than the one-quarter Irving allowed, but a wholesaler like Carey had to give one-fifth to his retailers. In August, 1822, when Wiley was trying to negotiate with Carey for a large order for the third edition of *The Spy* and for the forthcoming *Pioneers*, Carey wrote him that, with his (Carey's) book monopoly in many small towns, he could easily sell two thousand copies of *The Pioneers*, but that with the discount so small on quantity orders he would make seven hundred and fifty do.[16] He urged that Wiley sell whole editions at large discounts to two or three booksellers, each of whom would control a large retail territory without competition. This was Carey's scheme for meeting British literary competition on behalf of the American author and publisher, and it might have worked —for a while. Obviously, however, discounts that were too low to encourage either middlemen like Carey, or his country retailers, prevented the wide distribution that Cooper might have profited by. But Cooper took the short view. Announced at the height of *The Spy's* popularity, *The Pioneers* was sold out to retailers six months before publication, and on the day it appeared —February 1, 1823—3500 copies had been sold by seven participating New York booksellers before noon. The author saw no reason to increase the discount on a book so readily salable.

But by 1825, he had learned not to be his own publisher. The contract for *Lionel Lincoln*,[17] which gave Wiley the right to print and publish ten thousand copies within one year, the author receiving five thousand dollars, marks a turning point. The document states that the publishers were to pay for all printings within fourteen days by promissory notes "which shall be obtained from the sale of said work. . . ." The publishers, therefore, were to pay the cost of manufacture, which they could do on credit, but Cooper was to receive his money only as fast as it was paid in by booksellers. The most interesting fact is that the arrangement called for a reduction in Cooper's profit to twenty-five per cent. The difference between this and the thirty-six per cent he apparently got for *The Pilot* was the amount he was willing to pay to get rid of the nuisance of managing and financing manufacture. But the difference was theoretical. If only six thousand copies were printed, Cooper's profit would still be five thousand dollars—at a rate of over forty per cent.

His next book and all others until 1844 were to be "published," in every sense of the word, by the competent house of Carey. I have told the rest of that story elsewhere,[18] but I shall repeat here what seems to me to be the essence of Cooper's professional rise and decline. His rise was directly related to the fact that for the first time a publisher was willing to take small profits for the sake of the prestige of an author's name. Until the mid-thirties, the Careys managed to give Cooper the equivalent of a royalty of up to forty-five per cent, break even themselves on a sale of five thousand, and make a profit of six per cent if they sold fifty-five hundred. His decline was directly geared to the reprint competition which drove down retail prices. In 1826, the *Mohicans* sold for two dollars, sales were 5750, Cooper's rate was forty-three per cent, and his returns were $5000. Sixteen years later, in 1842 when the bottom was dropping out of retail book prices, his *Wing and Wing* sold for fifty cents, sales were 12,500, his rate was twenty per cent, and his returns less than $1,200. Thus, though sales of the later book were more than twice that of the earlier, his returns were less than one-fourth.

Irving's decline was not quite as precipitous, because by 1829, the year Carey became his publisher, he had shifted to the field of history and biography, in which the reprint competition was less disastrous than in fiction. Between then and 1841, his income ranged from

$7000 in productive years, to a steady $1150 a year when he was being paid only for leases on his old works. But his books were out of print from 1841 to 1848—and for the same reason that brought the Carey-Lea dynasty's distinguished literary publishing career to an end.

The new era began about 1848-50. Competition had killed off many of the reprinters; respectable publishers made agreements not to interfere with each other's reprint arrangements; and the regular reprinting of British novels in *Harper's Monthly* put the whole business on a new basis. Retail book prices rose to a level where some profit was possible. The extension of railroads into the interior opened up a truly national market for which publishers could produce in quantity, and enterprising firms began to accumulate the capital which enabled them to take over their proper functions from writers. The literary gains of the preceding era were consolidated, so to speak, when publishers like Putnam of New York issued collected editions of the works of established authors like Cooper and Irving (the latter had an annual income from Putnam of $8000); and Ticknor & Fields began to gather up the work of American poets in complete editions.

But above all, writers began to trust publishers to do the whole job of publishing for them and were thus relieved of the commercial busy-work which many of them detested. Publishing had finally become a profession in which every detail, from manufacturing to promotion and publicity, was managed by experts.

Yet, in making these gains, writers lost some of the independence which had been possible when they had more control over publishers. As publishers became stronger, and interpreted more accurately the public taste, they encouraged writers to cater to that taste, and to behave like producers of a commodity. Carey & Lea, the ablest of American publishers before 1850, and the shrewdest interpreters of the public, had exercised precisely such influence on Cooper, suggesting again and again that he write this or not write that. Usually he did as he pleased, but they (or the public they represented) tended to keep fiction inside the conventional bounds of the diverting romance, and to discourage experiment.

In the new era, such pressures on the writer gradually intensified. In particular, the demand for novels increased enormously, and when *Harper's Monthly,* begun in 1850, put serialization on a firm basis, the lure of double pay for two forms of publication drew into the field of the novel many writers who had little natural aptitude for it.

Hawthorne's career is a case in point. He had learned that short fiction was relatively unprofitable, and that collections of tales were commercially almost valueless. He had tried five times in twenty-five years to circumvent this fact by setting a group of tales in a framework which would make them resemble a novel, but publishers were not interested. The last of these attempts came in 1849, when he planned a collection called "Old Time Legends," one of the legends being a novelette called *The Scarlet Letter.* James T. Fields changed the course of Hawthorne's whole career by persuading him to expand the novelette and publish it separately: it had a sale of six thousand in a year, and Hawthorne never wrote another short story.

For the rest of his life he was completely dependent on Ticknor & Fields. They were his bankers, his purchasing agents, and, unwittingly, his exploiters. They paid him top royalties, published everything he submitted, urged him to write more, and never drew up a contract or even a complete statement of sales. They were honest, and they had generous faith in a writer who, in spite of his reputation with critics, had never been really popular. But probably they contributed to his eventual crackup by encouraging him to overproduce.

On the sound business principle that an author's name is a commodity, and that the public forgets a commodity of which it is not constantly reminded, Fields always liked to have a new Hawthorne book ready to float before the wave of the previous book's sale had flattened out; and if no new work was ready, he had Hawthorne prepare a new edition of an old one. Thus, in his first three and a half years with the firm, he got out seven new books and two new editions—an average of one title every five months. The records show that Hawthorne's reward for all this was only $1500 a year—infinitely better than he had ever done before, but who could keep up such a pace? He took a consulship at Liverpool.

Yet he knew that he would have to go back to writing, and that the novel was the only literary form by which he could support himself professionally. How was a natural-born, short story writer to write novels in quantity? He had always worked in depth, not in breadth, through unity, not variety, through single tones rather than symphonic effects, through single, central incidents rather than through complex plots. These methods were appropriate to the tale, but difficult to sustain on a larger scale. Hawthorne himself did not believe that his characteristic unity of tone and singleness of purpose were an asset in the novel. Thus, he had argued for publishing *The Scarlet Letter* as part of a collection because, "Keeping so close to its point as the tale does, and diversified no otherwise than by turning different sides of the same dark idea to the reader's eye, it will weary very many people. . . . Is it safe, then," he asked his publishers, "to stake the fate of the book entirely on this one chance? A hunter loads his gun with a bullett [sic] and several buckshot. . . . [Similarly] it was my purpose to conjoin one long story with several shorter ones, so that, failing to kill the public outright with my biggest and heaviest lump of lead [I might hit them] with some of the buckshot."[19]

This "buckshot" theory of Hawthorne's was one of the reasons why he had tried for so many years to publish collections. And this was the reason why in the early fifties he had refused all offers for serialized novels. "In all my stories . . ." he wrote one editor, "there is one idea running through them like an iron rod." If this idea were "dragged slowly before the reader" for weeks and months, he said, "it would become intolerably wearisome." By contrast, he pointed out, the serial productions of Dickens and Thackeray "are distinguished by a great variety of scene and multiplicity of character, and the story is carried on through many threads of interest. . . ."[20]

Yet his greatest problem as a novelist was not lack of variety but lack of talent for rendering the naturalistic detail which was needed for the kind of novel the public wanted—detail descriptive of houses, streets, cities, people, incidents. Finding it difficult to invent such detail, he had kept notebooks in which he recorded masses of dull details concerning people, places, incidents. These he had used sparingly in his tales, but as a novelist he was dependent on them. For each novel after *The Scarlet Letter* he drew more heavily on his notes: at least half of his last one, *The Marble Faun*, was guidebook detail lifted out of his Italian notebooks. In the Preface to his English travel book, *Our Old Home*, he said, "These and other sketches were intended for the side scenes and exterior adornment of a work of fiction"—a work which he never completed because he could not control the plot.

The causes of Hawthorne's premature death are not clear, but as surely as in the case of Scott Fitzgerald his art suffered a crackup which helped to kill him. Fields had been putting pressure on him for several years for a new novel, and had even gone so far as to announce the coming serialization of a new work. Hawthorne finally made him withdraw the announcement, saying, ". . . too great an effort [to finish this book] will be my death. . . . I should smother myself in mud of my own making."[21] His publisher attended his burial three months later. In a sense, the smothering mud was his own notebooks. Under the economic necessity of writing more novels than he had in him, he began to rely more and more on his notes, and seemed to be less and less able to build anything out of them. In his last phase, the notes dominated the writing: he was trying to create ideas and situations which would make the stored-up details in his notebooks usable. This, it seems to me, is one explanation of the tragic mess of unfinished novels which he left behind him when he died.

To blame his death on his well-meaning publisher or on the appetites of readers would be false and sentimental. Fiction, after all, is one of the most public of literary arts; and though the truly creative novelist always has the private vision of the poet, he must, if he wants to be professional, find a surface formula acceptable to that middle-brow culture to which our literary publishing has been attuned ever since it came to maturity in the middle of the last century. Hawthorne and Melville could find no such formula, and so went down to different kinds of defeat. It would be hard to deny that the discovery and accurate appraisal of the middle range of American public taste by such acute publishers as Carey, the Harpers, and Ticknor & Fields, were a mixed and dubious blessing.

3

LITERARY GENRES AND ARTIFACTS

In our time, the packaging of products has become
—not a science (the word is much too readily applied
to processes which are merely technological), nor an
art (the successful package may be a horror to the
eye), but a skill which supports a twelve-billion-dollar
industry; and the idea of engineering the shapes of
things for the purpose of endowing them with the
appearance of social prestige has become an obsession
with the makers of cars, cigarettes, and whiskey. The
idea is, of course, anything but new. It was certainly
a factor in the manufacture of books in the early nineteenth century; and the physical appearance of the
literary artifact engages our interest the more because
it was *not* determined by market surveys, but reflected
an interplay between imported publishing customs and
social attitudes toward literature on the one hand, and
changing conditions in our native culture on the other.

The subject is extraordinarily complicated. If we
speculate on the implications of the wide margin, for
example, we cannot stop with Veblen's theory of con-
spicuous waste, though that is a good place to begin.
Veblen does not help much when we find, in Ticknor
& Fields's cost books,[1] that though a single edition of

Longfellow's poems was offered in as many as eight different bindings (dark paper, glazed paper, boards, plain cloth, cloth with gilt centre, cloth with full or extra gilt, and imitation morocco), his fictional works, and those of all other Ticknor authors including Hawthorne, were issued only in one binding—cloth. But if one is tempted to conclude on this basis alone that the social status of poetry was superior to that of fiction, one had better note that Longfellow permitted other publishers to print cheap and tawdry double-column, paper-covered editions of his verse.

The literary artifact reflected complex attitudes not only of the writer toward his own work, but his conception of public attitudes toward him and toward literature; and all these attitudes were conditioned by tradition and custom. Although, for three decades before Scott, critical opinion put the novel at the very bottom of the literary scale, we note that most editions of *Charlotte Temple* before 1820 were bound in leather, or wooden boards, which suggests that this piece of early soap opera was not thought of as ephemeral diversion. But perhaps such binding means only that cloth and cardboard binding had not yet been developed to the point of profitable mass production.[2] Carey offered his first Philadelphia edition (1794) of *Charlotte* "sewed" and unbound for five shillings. Does this mean that many or most purchasers ordered cheaper bindings, or no binding at all, and that only the leather-covered ones have survived?

Literary criticism in the early nineteenth century indicates that the essay, history, biography, and poetry (especially the epic) were the genres held in highest

esteem, contemporary fiction and drama[3] the lowest.
I begin with poetry.

A letter by Joel Barlow in 1783 to Elias Boudinot,
president of the Continental Congress, urging the necessity of a national copyright law, reveals something
about the relation between the artifact and the social
status of the epic genre.

> There is now a Gentleman in Massachusetts
> who has written an Epic Poem, entitled "The Con-
> quest of Canaan," a work of great merit. . . . It
> has lain by him, finished, these six years, without
> seeing the light; because the Author cannot risque
> the expences of publication, sensible that some
> ungenerous Printer will immediately seize upon
> his labors, by making a mean & cheap impression
> [edition], in order to undersell the Author and
> defraud him of his property.
>
> This is already the case with the Author of
> McFingal [John Trumbull]. This work is now re-
> printed in an incorrect, cheap edition; by which
> means the Author's own impression lies upon his
> hands, & he not only loses the labor of writing &
> the expence of publishing, but suffers in his reputa-
> tion by having his work appear under the disadvan-
> tages of typographical errors, a bad paper, a mean
> letter & an uncooth page, all which were necessary
> to the printer in order to catch the Vulgar by a low
> price.[4]

Two key words in this letter are "Gentleman" and
"the Vulgar," indications that when American literary
culture began, our writers thought of literature and
authorship in terms of that British aristocratic tradition
which assumed that belles-lettres was a class commod-

ity, produced by and for the elite, but presumptuously appropriated by the vulgar. The words "cheap" and "uncooth" are also signs of a carry-over. In England, where for two centuries the vulgar had consumed sensational pamphlets and broadsides, badly printed on poor paper, the upper classes associated "good" literature with expensive format; concomitantly, a cheap format was the natural dress of cheap content. But note the implication of Barlow's statement that the Vulgar were buying a cheaply printed *epic*: the assumption of a necessary relation between content and format was beginning to break down (though, as we shall see, it persisted for many more decades), and the era of cheaply printed "good" literature was now forecast, if not begun. Though Barlow's professional psychology was essentially patrician, twenty-four years after this letter he compromised with the elite tradition. When, in 1807, he published his revised epic as *The Columbiad*, he reaffirmed his old belief in a necessary relation between belles-lettres and the upper class by putting ten thousand dollars into the manufacture of what was declared to be the most sumptuously printed volume thus far produced in America. But simultaneously he issued it in two cheaper grades of paper "in an effort to reach various levels of the public."[5] Of course, he had become, by 1807, not only a republican but a rich man. As we shall see, his case offers interesting parallels with that of a later patrician poet, Henry Wadsworth Longfellow.

Until the egocentric work of the Keats-Shelley-Poe school drove a wedge between poetry and the general reader, verse continued, in the nineteenth century, to have the high cultural status it had enjoyed in the eighteenth century. It was a common mode of public expression, and an accepted form for religious, moral, and satirical discourse. College students were required to write it regularly, and vied for the honor of reciting commencement poems. It was used widely in newspapers and magazines—not only as filler, but as primary material. Editors never paid for it because the supply was unlimited: everybody wrote it. Odes were written for every important public celebration. Theater managers ordered verse prologues and epilogues for new plays. Newspaper carriers presented their customers with verses especially written for Christmas.

But all this does not mean that the living poet, or anyone else who made the writing of belles-lettres his primary occupation, was respected; at any rate, such writers *felt* that they were condescended to by the public. The Elizabethan upper-class, says Phoebe Sheavyn, the historian of the literary profession in the Renaissance, loved poetry but despised the professional poet who was in any way dependent on his craft. ("Thou call'st me Poet, as a term of shame," wrote Ben Jonson to "My Lord Ignorant.")[6] From that day to this, there has been an extreme ambivalence in the public's attitude—on the one hand, veneration (even by those who never read anything) for great names like Homer and Milton, and for old living poets who have made a reputation; and on the other hand, contempt (expressed in such historic phrases as "beggarly poet" and "wretched rimester") for young and unsuccessful poets. The situation got worse in the nineteenth century when the public conceived a hostile image of the Romantic lyric poet, imputing to him not only poverty, but impracticality, temperamentality, effeminacy, immorality, and a feeling of superiority to ordinary mortals.

In the second and third decades, this image was both confirmed and modified by Byron, whose career stirred American poets and publishers to the realization that the public would not only read contemporary verse but pay extraordinary sums for it. But British facts were not American facts, and it was to take America several more decades to produce a professional poet who could change the public's attitude toward native poetry, and publishers who could turn out an appropriate and profitable artifact as its vehicle.

That man was Longfellow—not Bryant, not Poe, not Emerson, not Holmes, because, other reasons apart, they were lyric poets who simply could not build up a stock of short poems in large enough quantity to constitute a professional commodity. (The total verse output of a Bryant or a Poe could be put into one thin volume.) Long narratives had provided the necessary bulk for Byron, and were to do so for Longfellow, eighty per cent of whose verse was in some form of story. Moreover, his verse stories were predominantly historical, and, as we shall see, history, in one form or another, was the chief substance of most successful writing before 1850, no matter what the literary genre.

What is not generally realized about Longfellow's contribution, however, is the way in which he, systematically and patiently, changed the American reader's attitude toward poetry. For twenty-five years, from 1824 to 1849, he propagandized his readers before he was fully satisfied that they accepted him and it. The buyer of his verse probably was not aware that he was reading poems that advertised poets and poetry, yet Longfellow was one of the most successful of all promoters of the art. Such promotion was by no means new; in England it had become common by the seventeenth century, and earlier. But by the 1840's the American cultural situation had made the defense of poetry a psychological necessity for those who wrote it. A large majority of Longfellow's poems contain some favorable reference to poetry, poets, artists, art, scholars, or literature in general. Bards are sublime, grand, immortal; singers are sweet, songs are beautiful, art is wondrous, books are household treasures. Hans Sachs is remembered after Kaisers are forgotten; Michelangelo is impudent to cardinals; John Alden, the scholar, wins out over Miles Standish, the man of action. Poetry is identified with the natural and the familiar, with the great organic processes of nature, rather than with the exotic or the intellectual. Birds, flowers, and children are poems, as are seaweed, horses, the wind, and hearthfire. By 1849, he felt satisfied that he was accepted by the common reader and that he had elevated the public status of his art.

He built this campaign on the foundation of two beliefs, lacking either of which he would have failed. First, a belief in the exalted function of poetry in civilization—any civilization. This conviction was buttressed by another: that poetry is inseparable from learning and scholarship, as indeed it has been, from Virgil and Dante to Pound and Eliot. He knew that the public has always accorded the most respect, however reluctantly, to those poets who *know* something—

languages, history, religions—and he lost nothing in reputation by being a professor of foreign languages and literatures at Harvard, a fact which his verse does not conceal.

In the second place, he was fully aware of the public's latent hostility to poets and thus was able to cope with it. In the beginning he was merely defensive. In *Outre-Mer*, his prose "sketch book" of 1835, he was as nervous as Irving had been about the public's scorn of the imaginative writer. The anonymous first-person speaker begins by supinely begging the "Worthy and Gentle Reader's" indulgence; is conscious that the reader is "busy" and thanks him for wasting his valuable time; and ends by feeling sorry for himself and for the little book which the "busy world" will soon forget.

The most promising part of this sorry jumble of a book seems completely irrelevant to its total design: it is his own review of Sir Philip Sidney's *Defense of Poetry*, which he had contributed to the *North American Review* in 1832. Throughout the review throbs Longfellow's awareness that the busy public thinks of poetry as "effeminate nonsense" or dangerous moonshine injurious to the life of action, and of the "vocation of the poet" as something beneath the contempt of active men. But the book also contains defenses upon which Longfellow was to build his own career as poet. Poets *have been* men of action—useful men; and Longfellow was a useful citizen in the teaching career which he had just begun. And poetry *is* useful, not only in its adherence to "the truth of nature," but for its instruc-

tion in the culture of other nations which can lift men
out of their provincial ignorance.

His prose romance *Hyperion*, four years later, is a
thinly disguised attempt to make the poet publicly
respectable. By this date, his position is firmer. He
does not beg the reader's indulgence; indeed, he puts
him on the defensive in the very first sentence by tell-
ing him that he is a "fool" if he asks the author to
define the word "poet." And he takes the offensive
against the world's conception of the poet as effeminate
by describing his hero in aggressively masculine terms:
Paul Flemming resembles Harold, the Fair-Hair, of Nor-
way, otherwise known in Icelandic song as Regner
Hairy-Breeches, who was always getting into mischief
with maidens and handsome widows. A travelogue
through Central Europe motivates the two main char-
acters to discourse that has more edge than anything
else Longfellow wrote in his life. The two defend the
life of the scholar, the poet, the musician, and the
artist. Next to the Newgate Calendar, they agree, "the
most sickening chapter in the history of man" is the
world's treatment of authors. Indirectly, Longfellow
draws the reader into an attitude of respect for art
by associating magnificent scenes and historic names
with literary works, and by disguising as dialogues his
old classroom lectures on German artists and poets,
illustrating them with translations from their verse.

Most important of all, however, is a line of argument
by the hero which suggests why Longfellow never suffered the American poet's usual fate of alienation from
the public. Every defense of the artist's and scholar's

way of life is accompanied by a concession to the public's prejudices. A plea for scholars is followed by an attack on the evils of excessive scholarly seclusion from the world of men, and by a caricature of the kind of scholar who wants to "die with a proof-sheet in [his] hand." Sorrow for the "calamities of authors" is balanced with the confession that many of them have "false and exaggerated ideas of poetry and the poetic character," that they disdain "common sense," and that they wrongfully "keep aloof from their fellow men." Goethe is great, they agree—and very much like Ben Franklin—but too sensual. France is quaint, but modern French writers are obscene. A lecture on the New Philosophy of Fichte is followed by a discussion that sounds like an attack on the New Criticism in our own time.

Especially interesting is the fact that in this book Longfellow commits himself to a kind of poetry attractive to the women of his day. The heroine, who is a target less for the hero's love than for his verse, is the new American middle- and upper-class woman, educated in academies in numbers exceeding those of men, in courses more closely related to the arts than to the practical sciences. She has time to read and travel, and she has been trained to emote. When after hearing the hero's translation of a German lyric, "she turned away to hide her tears," she responded precisely like the female readers of Longfellow's first volume of verse which was published this same year of 1839.

But a female audience was not enough for him. Since 1838 he had been yearning to be heard by the man in the street. Middle-class magazines in New York and

Philadelphia were giving him a circulation and reputation he could not get in New England, but he wished
to reach the masses. Early in 1840 he announced that
he had "broken ground in a new field . . . *The National
Ballad*. . . . I am going to have ["The Wreck of the
Hesperus"] printed on a sheet, and sold like *Varses*,
with a coarse picture on it. I desire a new sensation,
and a new set of critics." Hawthorne, whose sense of
humor was better than Longfellow's, was "tickled to
death with the idea," and promised to distribute the
sheet to skippers at the Custom House; but Professor
Felton of Harvard told his colleague quietly, "I
wouldn't."[7] Though the ballad was not printed as a
broadside, it did appear in a crude, wretchedly printed,
"mammoth newspaper," the *New World*, one of the
new mass media of the time. (Recall, at this point,
Barlow's words, fifty-seven years earlier—"a mean letter
& an uncooth page . . . to catch the Vulgar by a low
price.")

At Harvard, in 1840, two ancient traditions of verse-
making came to incredible confluence in an American
poet: that of the balladmonger and his broadside, and
that of the scholarly gentleman-poet of the coterie.
The broadside mood proved to be temporary, but the
typography and format of Longfellow's works between
1838 and 1846 show what democracy had done to
poetry since Barlow's time, and what had to happen
before Ticknor & Fields could find the right formats
at the right prices for a stabilized poetry market. At
the very moment when the *New World* was selling on
the New York newsstands for twelve and one-half cents,
Longfellow's first collection, *Voices of the Night*, con-

taining a scant two dozen lyrics, elegantly printed on
fine paper, with wide margins, was being bought in
Boston bookstores for seventy-five cents. These and
succeeding small volumes throughout the forties were
also re-issued in expensive large-paper editions, copies
of which the author presented to ladies and gentlemen
of Boston and Cambridge society. But in the same
period he permitted a Boston mass-audience publisher
of cheap fiction to issue a miserable little edition in
pamphlet form, on poor paper, for twelve and a half
cents. In the same year, a Philadelphia house brought
out his collected poems, sumptuously illustrated, at
from $3.50 to $7.00 a copy for the carriage trade. And
six months later, Harper of New York issued a double-
column, paper-covered pamphlet edition at fifty cents.
For almost five years, these two editions, at fifty cents
and seven dollars, were the only available "complete
poems" of Longfellow, and for five years he tried to
find out where he belonged between these two economic—and presumably cultural—extremes. When the
Western market eagerly absorbed Harper's fifty-cent
volume, he knew that the people were reading him,
but there was little dignity or profit in such editions.
The reception of the luxury editions showed that people
respected what they had to pay handsomely for—a
point that Robert Frost has been making for a long
time. It remained for Ticknor & Fields to find the
middle ground of both price and taste.

The rest of the Longfellow story centers in the problem of the modern epic, which is too complex for
extended treatment here. From Barlow to Ezra Pound,
our leading poets (Emerson and Emily Dickinson

are the major exceptions) have been dissatisfied with
the lyric, and have sought a modern equivalent of the
European epic—a form capable of carrying the weight
of a major idea or subject. Poe's *Eureka* was such an
attempt, as was *Leaves of Grass* in its final form. So
was Longfellow's *Christus,* a dramatic trilogy which
was such a complete failure that this, the most popular
poet in the world, spent his last years writing verse
which argued that the artist's reward is in his labor,
not in his achievement.

William Gilmore Simms recognized the problem
when he said in the Preface to his novel *The Yemasee*
that "the modern Romance is the substitute . . . for
the ancient epic." He was wrong, of course, for the
distinguishing characteristic of the epic was that it
subsumed the life of a whole nation or a people or a
religion. By 1850, it had become impossible for any
Western poet to sum up his nation's culture in an epic,
and certainly no American romantic novelist ever succeeded. Cooper might have come close to creating an
epic of frontier life if he had planned the Leather-
stocking quintet as a coherent unit from the start,
instead of jerry-building it.

But the romantic novel was doomed from the beginning—for two reasons, among others. First, a publishing
tradition, namely the two-volume format, imposed arti-
ficial limits upon its length, and thus, to some extent,
predetermined its structure. Second, the public had—
and has—a deep-seated suspicion of make-believe fiction, and a strong appetite for true-to-life fiction. This
explains why the realistic and naturalistic novel has
been overwhelmingly dominant for the last hundred

years. Before 1850, the romantic novel was accepted precisely to the extent that it attached itself to history, which is, of course, another form of true-to-life narrative.

History per se (and I include here the allied forms of biography, and of travel, which is a kind of contemporary history) was the first genre to be successfully established on a profitable professional basis. It had tremendous social prestige because it was useful and educational, and because its methods were in accord with the reigning Scottish common-sense philosophy, which celebrated actuality and denigrated possibility. It is not surprising that in the massive critical onslaught on fiction before Scott and Cooper, the reading of history was recommended as an antidote to the novel.

The Jared Sparks papers at Harvard show that by the 1830's that historian was making a small industry out of the lives and letters of Washington and Franklin, and his *Library of American Biography*; and that he had traveling agents distributing these all over the South and West at a time when most New England books (except school texts and juveniles) stayed home.[8] When in this same decade, Bancroft, Prescott, and Irving made history-writing an art, history became the most remunerative of all the genres (excluding the historical novels of Cooper). Every major publisher in the country bid for Prescott's works, which were issued in luxurious formats. During the reprint competition of the forties, history suffered less than any other literary form. It is no wonder, then, that the most successful

writers of the time were those who made alliances
with history and other kinds of factual narrative. One
can measure many a literary fortune of the day by
the extent to which the writer appropriated a historical
mode. Cooper, for example, was almost always successful when he stayed within the historical frame, and
almost always got into trouble with the public when
he deserted it for social criticism. Melville's books were
acclaimed and bought when they were solidly based
on his travels, and abused and neglected when he
moved into the world of possibility.

The most interesting case is that of Washington
Irving, whose career illuminates our small knowledge
of the history of the sociology of authorship. Let us
charge off his *History of New York* in 1809 as a kind
of freak, although it is proof of the early vogue of
historical writing. The sale of the first edition, probably
3750 copies, was huge for a three-dollar book, and
Irving made an unprecedented $3000 on it.

His planned career began in 1819. He was to be a
writer of light belles-lettres—of essays and tales meant
for diversion. He kept this role for five years and three
books—*The Sketch Book, Bracebridge Hall,* and *Tales
of a Traveller.* The first was a great success, the second
less so, and the third came close to failure. Looking
around for a more dependable genre, he chose history,
partly because in England, where he was living, the
huge earnings of Gibbon, Robertson, and Hume had
become legendary and had helped to make the writing
of history a thriving profession. Considering the fact
that the *Voyages of Columbus,* his first historical work

after *Tales of a Traveller*, earned him over $25,000, it is no wonder that after 1824 he wrote no book that was not essentially historical or biographical.

But money was not the only cause for his shift. From the beginning, he had felt guilty as a creative writer. Like the poet, the tale writer felt himself to be a social deviate: from the point of view of the man of action, he was nonproductive, an idler. Hawthorne summed it up in the Introduction to *The Scarlet Letter* when he imagined his Puritan ancestors contemplating his vocation and asking, "What is he? . . . A writer of story-books! What kind of a business in life . . . may that be? Why, the degenerate fellow might as well have been a fiddler!" There is a hidden autobiography in Hawthorne's earliest pieces which reveals the pain he experienced when he discovered the world's contempt for his kind of life.

There are similar revelations in Irving's works before he became a historian. In his statements about himself and his writings, the most frequently reiterated word is *mere*. "My talents are merely literary," "I am a mere belles-lettres writer," "my works of mere imagination." Other phrases confirm the import of the adjective: my works are "light and trifling," and "lacking in scope," my instrument is a mere "flute," I have "no lofty theme." The address to the "Worthy Reader" in *Brace-bridge Hall* is an apology for writing light, "pleasant" sketches. And the Preface to *Tales of a Traveller* is a deplorable piece of condescension to his own craft: stranded in Germany, and too sick to read a book, he will write one—a mere matter of "rummaging around in one's portfolio." But in this piece there is also an augury of his professional future—a reference to the world's awe of and reverence for "the labors of the learned."

Irving's pseudonyms, and other intermediaries which he puts between himself and his tales, appear to be a defense against the "Worthy Reader" who liked stories but was contemptuous of storytellers. These devices mean in effect: Don't equate me with Geoffrey Crayon, Gent.; but if you do, please note that Crayon does not actually tell stories; he merely reports them as told to him by someone you can really condescend to—funny old Diedrich Knickerbocker, or "the Nervous Gentleman," or a fat Dutchman—just as you have always condescended to the nursemaid who puts you to sleep with fairy tales.

The transition to a kind of history that suited his talents was not easy. Though the great Spanish scholar, Navarrete, had done most of the spade-work for him in his recently published documents of the Spanish voyages of discovery, Irving's two years of labor at turning the materials into an accurate but readable life of Columbus almost killed him. What he needed was a formula which would free him from the responsibilities of the historian and allow for the play of imagination, yet keep him within the profitable and respectable pale of history. *The Conquest of Granada*, which he had begun as a relief from the boredom of scholarship in the very midst of the writing of *Columbus*, was just such an experiment. He hoped *Granada* would be regarded as a new kind of history, as a narrative in "an entertaining and popular form, without sacraficing [sic] the intrinsic truth of history . . . all being dressed up with an eye to the scenery of the country and the customs of the time," and "over the whole a colouring that may give it something of the effect of a work of the imagination"[9]—in short "romantic history" as opposed to "historical romance."

Yet his old reluctance to use his own name in light literary works persisted. *Granada* carried a new pseudonym—"Fray Antonio Agapida." The unsigned Preface describes him as an old Spanish monk whose manuscripts, dispersed in the late wars, form the basis of the narrative. To avoid making Protestant judgments on Catholic history (a dilemma which Prescott faced honestly in his histories of the Spanish empire), Irving called the friar a "good old orthodox chronicler," and cited as additional sources three actual Spanish historians whose piety was similarly denominational. But primarily, Fray Agapida serves to relieve Irving of the blame for an unscholarly mixture of fact and myth, and for the tedious chronicling of endless identical battles.

The results were confusing. In America, some people may have been taken in by the prefatory statement that Agapida's manuscripts might be seen in the library of the Escorial, but there were many who realized that he was imaginary and read the volume as pure fiction. In England, the situation was worse. Murray outraged Irving by putting his name on the title page: "By so doing," wrote Irving, "you make me personally responsible for the verity of the facts and the soundness of the opinions of what was intended to be given as a romantic chronicle. I presume you have done this to avail yourself of whatever attractions my name might have in drawing attention to the work; but this might

have been effected in some other way, without med-
dling with the work itself."[10] How complex was the
psychology of pseudonymity: in American editions
Irving's name was printed on the reverse of the title
page as the copyrighter of the work!

Thereafter, he shifted back and forth from anonymity
or pseudonymity to his own name, according to the
nature of the work. *The Alhambra*, "by the author of
The Sketch Book," was a mixture of autobiography,
travel, and legend. *Astoria*, a not too crass glorification
of John Jacob Astor, who subsidized the book, was a
factual narrative which bore Irving's own name, as did
the *Adventures of Captain Bonneville* which was a
digest of a real captain's journals. In the three volumes
of the *Crayon Miscellany*, Irving returned for the last
time to his old pseudonym. But by that date, it was
hardly more than a commercial lure. Drawing on his
now well-known travels in Great Britain, Spain, and
the Far West, Irving presented the work as a mixture
of scenes and sketches "together with such other
themes, both real and imaginary, as may present themselves to the mind of the Author." The capitalized
reference to himself in the third person is the only
remaining vestige of his old nervousness about his
identity, and the books themselves contain straightfor-
ward, if slightly defensive, references to his other books,
his career, and the public's attitudes toward him. The
identification of Washington Irving with Geoffrey
Crayon was almost complete, and Irving now deserted
his old stand-in.

After the success of his *Life of Columbus*, Murray
of London suggested that his next book be "some light

work in [your] old vein." Irving admitted that he had some such things on hand, but "thought it best to hold them back until [he] had written a work or two of more weight, even though of less immediate popularity. A literary reputation, to hold well with the public," he continued, "requires some *make weights* of the kind. Some massier materials, which form a foundation; the lighter works then become ornaments and embellishments. Depend upon it, had I continued to write works merely like the Sketchbook, the public would have ceased to read them. One must prose and be tedious at times to get a name for wisdom with the multitude, that one's jokes may afterward pass current."[11] Such concern for his reputation in his time is understandable. As a professional writer he could rightly declare, "I am not one of those who appeal from the decision of contemporaries to the decision of posterity; for every work must be judged by the age for which it is written."[12] But his lack of respect for works that the public enjoyed and for the public that enjoyed them is obvious. A hundred years later the "multitude" was still reading such "jokes" as "Rip Van Winkle" and "The Legend of Sleepy Hollow," ignorant that Irving had ever been a historian. All his life he violated a cardinal principle—that, though a writer must not take himself too seriously, he must be serious about his craft.

Let us turn from the genre to the artifact. A shelf of Irving first editions tells the eye that most of his works were issued in two volumes, no matter whether they were collections of short pieces or larger units, and one wonders why. Wonder increases when we note that practically all the novels of professionals like Cooper, Simms, Bird, Paulding, and Sedgwick were in the two-volume format. (Miss Sedgwick said in 1841 that it had never occurred to her that there could be more or less than two volumes.) Further investigation shows that although this format was used somewhat in the 1790's, it became the norm about 1820 and remained so until about 1844, when a greater variety of format for fiction becomes evident. Still closer inspection shows that from the nineties to 1820 many very short novels, issued in one volume, state on the title page that they are in two volumes; and though these are paged continuously, a title page for volume two appears in the middle. Mrs. Rowson's *Charlotte Temple* is a representative case. Although I have not seen all American editions of this tiny book, it is a good guess that after Carey's first edition in 1794, which, like the first London edition of 1791, was in two separate volumes, almost all subsequent editions were in one volume, and of these a bare majority have title pages for two volumes. Almost all the editions published in the larger towns, like Philadelphia, New York, and Hartford are in this category. This makes no sense until we trace the origin of the custom to England. The recent Lauterbach article on "The Nineteenth Century Three Volume [British] Novel" shows that before Scott's *Waverley* set the pattern for the three-volume form, the English novel went through a two-volume phase in the 1790's.[13] In this period, American reprinters of British novels imitated the original form to the extent of pretending that a work was in two volumes, even though it was bound within a single pair of covers to save expense. Probably for the same reason, when three-volume novels became the vogue in England, American reprinters issued the same titles in two volumes.

In England, the printing of small novels in two separate volumes, and longer ones in three, was a product of bookseller collusion to keep the prices of books high. In America, such high prices were impossible. So was collusion among publishers because we had no London, but, instead, many widely scattered and competing publishing centers. Yet British influence somehow predetermined the two-volume length of the American novel as written by Cooper and his contemporaries.

There was, of course, no inherent literary or aesthetic advantage in this particular length, and its great disadvantage was not only that it encouraged the writer to pad his work and be long-winded, but that it hindered the development of genuine functionalism in fictional form. The novelist had a set amount of space to fill, and he managed his materials, expanding or contracting as necessary, to fill that space. This procedure determined the external structure of most of Cooper's novels. For each work, he borrowed a plot from the vast storehouse of European story-formula (most commonly, the separation and reunion of separated members of a family, or lovers). The plot provided him with an initial situation and a denouement. (He called this "mere machinery.") The space between he filled up with improvised and miscellaneous material—incident, description, facts, history, discourse, authorial commentary—much of which was only loosely related to the plot. Obviously, a fiction so written cannot be read as an integrated, organic whole, and it is futile for present-day critics to try to do so. Yet it was an appropriate method for a professional novelist who was committed to regular and rapid production, and who had a great deal to tell the world which he could not organize and dramatize in the shape of unified story.

I think this situation has some bearing on the fact that during the two-volume period no American novel had any real distinction in form and structure. One might argue that Shakespeare did pretty well when he worked under similar mechanical restrictions in using the five-act form, but then, he and his contemporaries wrote a lot of obviously padded plays.

The historical pattern, then, was this: Up to 1820, novels could be of any length, but there were no gifted writers to take advantage of this freedom. From 1820 to about 1844, novelists wore the two-volume strait jacket. By the latter date the competition to make cheaper books was undermining the two-volume convention because it was too expensive. By 1850, fictional form had returned to its original freedom, as far as length was concerned, and it was precisely at this time that we got such structured masterpieces as *Moby Dick* and *The Scarlet Letter*—the one three times as long as the other, but each issued in a single volume.

This freedom was to be short-lived, however. Novelists were measured for a new strait jacket as soon as magazine editors began to decree the length of serialized fiction. The publishing correspondence of James and Howells is one long argument with editors about how much space a novel would be allowed. It is a nice irony that James achieved a new structural mastery in his last and major phase only after magazine editors began to send him pink slips.

But it is just such tensions between writers and society that make literature what it is, and one suspects that if writers had complete freedom they would not know what to do with it.

———

NOTES

Chapter 1

1. Carey & Lea to Cooper, Jan. 16, 1832 (MS, Yale University Library).
2. This document was in the office of Harper and Brothers when I used it years ago.
3. H. F. Barnes, *Charles Fenno Hoffman* (New York, 1930), p. 271.
4. Lucile Clifton, "The Beginnings of Literary Culture in Columbus, Ohio, 1812-1840" (Unpublished doctoral dissertation, Ohio State University, 1948).
5. R. G. Albion, *The Rise of the Port of New York, 1815-1860* (New York, 1939).
6. J. W. Livingood, *The Philadelphia-Baltimore Trade Rivalry* (Harrisburg, 1947).
7. Margaret E. Martin, *Merchants and Trade of the Connecticut Valley, 1750-1820* (Northampton, Mass., 1939), p. 208.
8. *Ibid.*, p. 58.
9. In 1803, Caritat was sending his libraries up the Hudson, the Raritan, and Long Island Sound. G. G. Raddin, *Hocquet*

Caritat and the Early New York Literary Scene, (Dover, N. J., 1953), p. 33. He would hardly have missed the opportunity to exploit the populous Connecticut River Valley.

10. Carey & Lea to Cooper, Apr. 10, 1826 (microfilm owned by J. F. Beard).

11. Richard Shryock, "Philadelphia and the Flowering of New England," *Pennsylvania Magazine of History and Biography,* LXIV (July, 1940), 305-13.

12. The road-river route was from New York, up the Raritan River to New Brunswick by boat, across to Trenton by stage, down the Delaware River to Philadelphia by boat (Albion, p. 145). The *Philadelphia Directory* of 1820 states that between these two cities there were three daily coach and steamboat lines, three daily coach lines, nine other steamboat lines (some of these daily, and some part way by coach). There was only one packet line to Boston, but to Pittsburgh there were two lines, thrice weekly, one via New York, one via Harrisburg.

13. R. E. Spiller, *The Cycle of American Literature* (New York, 1955).

14. See Dorothy Blakey, *The Minerva Press, 1790-1820* (London, 1939).

15. June 7, 1844. This manuscript was in the Longfellow House in Cambridge when I used it.

16. Dennie to Tyler, Aug. 30, 1797. L. G. Pedder (ed.), *The Letters of Joseph Dennie, 1768-1812* (Orono, Maine, 1936).

17. "List of American Plays, 1665-1860," *A History of the American Drama from the Beginning to the Civil War* (New York, 1923).

18. Dennie, *Letters,* Sept. 6, 1799; May 20, 1800.

19. Edward Everett to J. P. Kennedy, June 26, 1820 (MS, Kennedy Papers, Peabody Institute Library). R. H. Dana, Sr., had most of the numbers of *The Idle Man* both printed and published in New York rather than, as he put it, in "such an out of the way place as Boston." Dana to Charles Wiley, Aug. 22, 1821 (MS, Massachusetts Historical Society).

20. Mary E. Dewey, *The Life and Letters of Catharine Maria Sedgwick* (New York, 1871), p. 203.

21. Samuel Longfellow, *Life of Henry Wadsworth Longfellow* (Boston, 1886), I, 267.

22. Henry A. Beers, *Nathaniel Parker Willis* (Boston, 1885), p. 99.

23. Hawthorne to E. A. Duyckinck, July 1, 1845 (From Professor Randall Stewart's copy of the MS).

24. Sept. 21, 1846. See also Apr. 26, 1844. R. L. Rusk (ed.), *The Letters of Ralph Waldo Emerson*, (New York, 1939), III, 350, 250.

25. L. H. Sigourney to James Munroe, Nov. 7, 1845 (MS, Yale University). In the early 1840's, Munroe had as many distinguished names on his list as any publisher in the country: Emerson, Hawthorne, Longfellow, Parker, Pierpont, Sedgwick, to say nothing of Coleridge, Carlyle, and Fichte. He also, at times, published such notable magazines as the *Dial*, the *North American Review*, and the *Christian Examiner*. A thorough study of his career might reveal what was wrong with Boston publishing before Ticknor & Fields. Apparently, he made little effort to sell his books outside of Massachusetts, and there were rumors about his reliability. Emerson referred to his "dubious reputation" with "some of the elect." See letters, in Rusk, of Apr. 24, 1844 and Sept. 10, 1846. See also Hawthorne's letters of Sept. 10, 1841 and Sept. 27, 1841, in Roswell Field (ed.), *The Love Letters of Nathaniel Hawthorne* (Chicago, 1907).

26. S. H. Fisher, *The Publications of Thomas Collier, Printer, 1784-1808* (Litchfield, Mass., 1933).

27. Figures compiled from Richard Gimbel, *Thomas Paine, A Bibliographical Check List* (New Haven, 1956).

28. Figures compiled from Charles Evans, *American Bibliography*.

29. Figures compiled from L. H. Wright, *American Fiction, 1774-1850* (San Marino, California, 1948).

30. Figures compiled from Agnes M. Sibley, *Alexander Pope's Prestige in America, 1725-1835* (New York, 1949). The same pattern obtains for Young's *Night-Thoughts*. See Henry Pettit, "A Check-List of Young's *Night-Thoughts* in America," *Publications of the Bibliographical Society of America*, XLVII (Second Quarter 1948), 150-56.

31. Figures compiled from Ruth Leonard, "A Bibliographical Evaluation of the Copyright Records for the United States District Court of Massachusetts, 1800-1809" (Unpublished Master's thesis, Columbia University School of Library Science, 1944); and J. H. Whitty, *A Record of Virginia Copyright Entries, 1790-1844* (Richmond: Virginia State Library, 1911).

32. Figures compiled from Frank P. Hill, *American Plays, 1714-1830* (Stanford, 1934).

33. *New York Times Book Review,* July 13, 1958.

34. C. T. Kindilien, *American Poetry in the Eighteen Nineties* (Providence, 1956).

35. Cummings & Hilliard's accountings for the printing and distribution of the *Poems* are in the Willard Phillips Papers, Massachusetts Historical Society.

36. The information in this and the next paragraph on the publications of Carey & Hart and H. C. Baird is from the manuscript cost books of these firms in the Historical Society of Pennsylvania.

37. These and other figures on fiction were compiled from Wright, *op. cit.*

CHAPTER 2

1. Publisher-author correspondence shows that literary economics has been in close accord with the economy of the nation. The literary historian can make use of the charts on the business cycle from the eighteenth century to the present in Leonard P. Ayres, *The Chief Cause of This and Other Depressions* (Cleveland Trust Co., 1935).

2. My figures on *Sketch Book* sales and profits are conjectural because the records are not complete. These estimates are based on all available printed sources, as well as on a mass of scattered manuscript material, much of it in the Carey archive in the Historical Society of Pennsylvania.

3. Data from the MS, "Letter Books of Ticknor & Fields" (Harvard College Library). See also W. S. Tryon and

William Charvat (eds.), *The Cost Books of Ticknor and Fields and Their Predecessors, 1832-1858* (New York, 1949).

4. Carey & Lea to Cooper, Feb. 20, 1834 (MS, Yale University Library).

5. Harper and Brothers to J. P. Kennedy, Nov. 2, 1835: "We usually share profits . . . equally. We publish for Miss Sedgwick, for Messrs. Paulding, Simms, Slidell, etc., upon these terms." (MS, Kennedy Papers, Peabody Institute Library).

6. Melville's royalty accountings from the Harpers are in the Harvard College Library.

7. Aug. 11, 1820 (MS, American Antiquarian Society).

8. Oct. 3, 1820 (MS, Historical Society of Pennsylvania).

9. May 5, 1820 (MS, Historical Society of Pennsylvania).

10. Jan. 17, 1815 (MS, New York Public Library).

11. Nov. 18, 1839. Maude Howe Elliott, *Uncle Sam Ward and His Circle* (New York, 1938), p. 256.

12. Dec. 24, 1821 (MS, Historical Society of Pennsylvania).

13. Figures compiled from various documents in Yale University Library and the Historical Society of Pennsylvania.

14. MS, Historical Society of Pennsylvania.

15. MS, Historical Society of Pennsylvania.

16. Aug. 6, 1822 (MS, Historical Society of Pennsylvania).

17. Nov., 1824 (MS, Yale University Library).

18. "Cooper as Professional Author," *James Fenimore Cooper, A Re-Appraisal* (Cooperstown, N. Y.: The New York State Historical Association, 1950).

19. Jan. 20, 1850 (MS, Harvard College Library).

20. Printed in *The Critic* (Jan. 17, 1885).

21. Feb. 25, 1864 (MS, Huntington Library).

CHAPTER 3

1. Tryon and Charvat, *op. cit.*

2. The evidence is not conclusive, but cardboard binding seems to have come into common use earlier in America than in England. That Cooper's novels, from the beginning in 1820,

were bound in boards suggests "common use" from that date. Joseph W. Rogers ("The Rise of American Edition Binding," *Bookbinding in America* [Portland, Maine, 1941] pp. 135-36), citing John Carter, Geoffrey Keynes, and Michael Sadleir, states that, in England, cloth (presumably on cardboard covers) was "first used practically and regularly . . . probably between 1822 or 1823 and 1825." R. D. Altick in *The English Common Reader* (Chicago, 1957), p. 278, states that in England "boards were first used extensively by the cheap series of 1828-1832." Rogers (p. 140) makes the interesting suggestion that in America boards were often used as a temporary binding to hold a book together until the purchaser decided whether to give it a library binding, but that binders began to cover this "temporary" binding with paper and, later, cloth. This development would be in accord with the American demand for lower costs than obtained in England.

Roughly, the history of the binding of Cooper's novels (and presumably of most American novels) is as follows: boards, 1820-36; cloth-covered boards, 1836-42; paper wrappers, 1842-50.

We shall know a great deal more about the status of the various genres when Jacob Blanck, who describes bindings meticulously, completes his *Bibliography of American Literature*.

3. The history of binding seems to support critical opinion. Separately printed plays were almost invariably issued in paper covers. This may have been so because plays were of pamphlet size, but one notes that a great many small volumes of verse were bound in boards.

4. T. A. Zunder, *The Early Days of Joel Barlow* (New Haven, 1934), p. 165.

5. Leon Howard, *The Connecticut Wits* (Chicago, 1943), pp. 321-22. Note Howard's suggestion that because the sumptuousness of the book was embarrassing to Barlow's "democratic professions" he implied in his prefatory letter that Robert Fulton was responsible, financially and otherwise, for the magnificence of the volume. It is interesting, also,

that the work carries no copyright notice—at a time when most commercially valuable books were given this legal protection. Does the omission imply a patrician reluctance on Barlow's part to confess that his epic was of any financial importance to him?

6. Phoebe Sheavyn, *The Literary Profession in the Elizabethan Age* (Manchester, 1909), p. 157.

7. Lawrance Thompson, *Young Longfellow (1807-1843)* (New York, 1938), p. 309.

8. "If you knew the activities of the Yankees, who provide School Books for the Union, you wd see that it is impossible to get a [school] book into circulation without great exertion." Henry Carey to Mathew Carey, undated letter, in David Kaser, *Messrs. Carey & Lea of Philadelphia* (Philadelphia, 1957), p. 51. My impression, from scattered correspondence, is that New England publishers overcame transportation difficulties in the schoolbook field by selling other firms the right to publish and sell a book in a particular area, or by selling them duplicate plates.

9. S. T. Williams, *The Life of Washington Irving* (New York, 1935), I, 344.

10. *Ibid.*, 346.

11. *Ibid.*, 345.

12. *Ibid.*, 344-45.

13. C. E. and E. S. Lauterbach, "The Nineteenth Century Three-Volume Novel," *Papers of the Bibliographical Society of America* (Fourth Quarter 1957), pp. 263-302. The Lauterbachs base their statistics on the bibliographies of Dorothy Blakey and Michael Sadleir. Statistics on the incidence of two- and three-volume novels in England are somewhat different in E. P. Morton's article in the *Nation* (Apr. 3, 1913), pp. 330-32, but Morton's figures cannot be checked.

INDEX

Alden, John, 67
Appleton Co., 35
Astor, J. J., 79

Baird, H. C., 35
Baltimore, Md., 19, 28, 45
Bancroft, George, 74
Barlow, Joel, 26, 28, 63, 64, 71, 72, 89
Benjamin, Park, 28
Bindings, 46, 62, 88–89
Biography, 54, 62, 73
Bird, R. M., 81
Boston, Mass., 19, 21, 23, 26–29, 31, 32, 34, 36, 45, 47, 50, 72
Boudinot, Elias, 63
Bradford & Inskeep, 50
Brook Farm, 21
Brooks, Van Wyck, 20, 28
Bryant, W. C., 22, 25, 34, 35, 36, 66
Byron, Lord, 17

Cambridge, Mass., 34
Capital, 19, 42, 44, 46, 50, 55
Carey, Mathew (and successors), 18, 19, 20, 24, 26, 35, 38, 39, 42, 43, 44, 47, 48, 49, 50, 52, 53, 54, 56, 60, 62, 81

Caritat, Hocquet, 20, 84
Channing, W. E., 28
Charleston, S. C., 49
Cincinnati, O., 17, 20, 29, 42
Cleveland, O., 17
Collier, Thomas, 30
Colman, Samuel, 51
Columbus, O., 19
Commission publishing, 29, 41, 43, 44, 48
Connecticut, 20, 26, 30
Consignment, 43
Contracts, 44, 53, 57
Cooper, J. F., 18, 20, 21, 22, 24, 35, 36, 38, 41, 43, 44, 49, 50–56, 73–75, 81, 82, 89
Copyright, 42, 63
Correspondents, 45, 47, 48, 49, 51
"Courtesy of the Trade," 40
Cozzens, J. G., 22
Credit, 45, 48, 51, 52, 53
Cummings & Hilliard, 87

Dana, R. H., Sr., 43, 85
Dante, 67
Dennie, Joseph, 20, 26, 28
Dickens, Charles, 58
Dickinson, Emily, 72

Discounts, 29, 39, 40–42, 46–49, 51–53
Disraeli, Benjamin, 50
Drama, 33, 63
Dryden, John, 21
Dumas, Alexandre, 24

Eliot, T. S., 67
Emerson, R. W., 23, 29, 30, 50, 66, 72, 86
Epic, 62, 63, 64, 73
Erie Canal, 19
Essay, 62, 75
Exchange system, 47

Fay, T. S., 18, 36
Felton, C. C., 71
Fichte, J. G., 70
Fields, J. T., 56, 57, 59
Fitzgerald, Scott, 59
Format, 40, 64, 71, 73, 74, 81
Franklin, Benjamin, 70, 74
Freneau, Philip, 21
Frost, Robert, 72

Gibbon, James, 75
Gift Books, 35
Goethe, J. W., 30, 70
Goldsmith, Oliver, 30
Graham's Magazine, 24, 35
Graves, Robert, 33
Gray, Thomas, 30
Griswold, R. W., 35
Half-profits system, 43
Harper & Brothers, 18, 19, 27, 34, 42, 44, 49, 60, 72
Harper's Monthly, 55, 56
Hartford, Conn., 19, 27, 30, 32, 81
Harvard University, 28, 67, 71

Hawthorne, Nathaniel, 23, 27, 29, 36, 42, 44, 56–60, 62, 71, 76, 83
History (as genre), 36, 54, 62, 66, 74–78, 82
Holmes, O. W., 66
Homer, 65
Howells, W. D., 83
Hudson River, 19
Hume, David, 75

Irving, Washington, 22, 36, 38, 39, 40–55, 63, 68, 74–80

James, Henry, 83
Jobbers, 45, 49
Jonson, Ben, 65

Keats, John, 64
Kennedy, J. P., 36, 88
Kindilien, C. T., 34
Knickerbockers, 21

Lauterbach, C. E. and E. S., 81
Livingood, J. W., 19
London, England, 21
Longfellow, H. W., 22, 25, 27, 28, 33–36, 42–44, 51, 62, 64–73
Lowell, J. R., 25, 27, 34

Mackenzie, Henry, 30
Marquand, J. P., 22
Massachusetts, 32, 33
Melville, Herman, 23, 37, 44, 60, 75, 83
Michelangelo, 67
Middletown, Conn., 20
Mills (of Charleston, S. C.), 49
Milton, John, 65

Minerva Press, 24
Monopoly, 46, 47, 52
Moore, Thomas, 50
Multiple imprints, 45, 46, 47
Munroe, James, 30, 86
Murray, John, 78, 79

Navarrete, M. F. de, 77
Newport, R. I., 31
New World, 71
New York, 19, 21–39, 45, 47–53,
    70, 81, 85
North American Review, 68

Ohio, 23, 30

Paine, Thomas, 31
Panic of 1837, 42
Paulding, J. K., 36, 49, 81, 88
Philadelphia, 19–38, 45, 48, 50,
    52, 71, 72, 81, 85
Poe, E. A., 23, 37, 44, 51, 64, 66,
    73
Poetry, 33, 34, 36, 55, 62–70
Pope, Alexander, 30, 32
Pound, Ezra, 20, 67, 72
Prescott W. H., 27, 43, 44, 74, 78
Printers, printing, 45, 49
Promotion, 55, 67
Providence, R. I., 31
Publicity, 46, 55
Putnam, G. H., 54

Quinn, A. H., 27

Remainders, 40
Reprints, 54, 55, 74
Retailing, 30, 34, 40, 45–49, 52–
    55
Richardson & Lord, 45

Richardson, Samuel, 31
Richmond, Va., 33
Risk (in publishing), 43–46
Robertson, William, 75
Robinson Crusoe, 31
Rowson, Mrs. S., 24, 31, 32, 62,
    81
Royalties, 40, 41, 44, 49, 54, 57

Sachs, Hans, 67
Salem, Mass., 47
San Francisco, Cal., 21
Sargent, L. M., 36
School texts, 74, 90
Scott, Walter, 17, 24, 40, 41, 49,
    50, 62, 74, 81
Sedgwick, Catharine, 28
Serials, 56, 58, 59, 83
Sheavyn, Phoebe, 65
Shelley, P. B., 64
Shryock, Richard, 20
Sidney, Philip, 68
Sigourney, L. H., 30
Simms, W. G., 73, 81, 88
Sparks, Jared, 74
Spengler, Oswald, 20
Spiller, R. E., 22, 24
Standish, Miles, 67
Stereotype plates, 19, 43, 46

Thackeray, W. M., 58
Theater, 27
Thomas, Moses, 39, 49
Thoreau, H. D., 23, 36
Ticknor & Fields, 27, 29, 35, 42,
    55, 57, 60, 61, 73, 77
Travel, 74
Trumbull, John, 63
Tyler, Royall, 25, 26

Van Winkle, C. S., 39, 45, 50

Veblen, Thorstein, 61
Virginia, 31, 32, 33

Walpole, N. H., 25
Ward, Samuel, 51
Weems, Parson, 24
Wells & Lilly, 47
Whitman, Walt, 73

Whittier, J. G., 27, 33
Wholesaling, 30, 39, 41
Wiley, Charles (and associates),
　21, 47, 48, 50–53
Willis, N. P., 28, 35, 36
Windsor, Vt., 32

Young, Edward, 86